W9-ACG-634

To the American Coast:
The Voyages and Explorations of M.S. Gvozdev,
the Discoverer of Northwestern America

By V.A. Divin

Translated by
Anatoli Perminov

Edited with an Introduction by
J.L. Smith

White Stone Press
Anchorage

Translation of
*K beregam Ameriki. Plavaniya
i issledovaniya M.S. Gvozdeva,
pervootkryvatelya Severo-Zapaknoy Ameriki*
Moscow, 1956
Whitestone Press, 3600 East 67th Avenue
Anchorage, Alaska 99507
English Translation 1997 by Whitestone Press
All Rights Reserved. Published 1997
Printed in the United States of America
ISBN: 09626727-1-8
LCCN:97-61615
Copyright 1997

"I do not require that a historian should narrate all he knows, nor even all that is true, because there are things that one should not narrate and which may be of doubtful interest, so that they should be hidden from the public..."[a]

G.F. Muller

Preface

This book is a translation of V.A. Divin's *K beregam Ameriki. Plavaniya i issledovaniya M. S. Gozdeva, pervootkryvatelya Severo-Zapadnoy Ameriki* published in Moscow by Geografgiz in 1956 on the 450th anniversary of the death of Christopher Columbus.

I first became interested in Alaska history when I was an undergraduate student. One of the requirements for graduation was either a course in Alaska Studies or Alaska History. I satisfied this requirement by taking a correspondence course in Alaska history from University of Alaska.

Later, while taking a graduate level course on the same subject, it became very clear to me that M. S. Gvozdev was the European discoverer of Alaska although there was very little written on the subject in English. After publishing an article on the Russian Discovery of Alaska in 1988 and an English translation of L.A. Goldenberg's 1985 biography of M.S. Gvozdev in 1990, I turned my attention to this volume.

I would like to gratefully acknowledge the assistance of Aaron Gray, Brian Branstetter, Phillip McGuire and especially my wife Phyllis who has graciously assisted me in virtually every endeavor I have undertaken these past 37 years. Surely, I have been blessed.

Published on the 265th anniversary of the Russian Discovery of Alaska.

August 21, 1997
Anchorage, Alaska

Table of Contents

Table of Maps and Illustrations

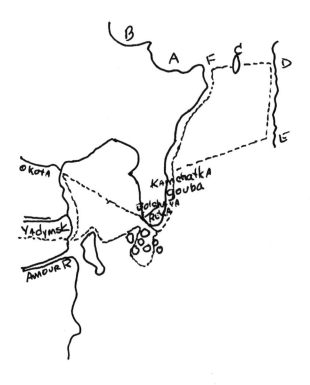

Delisle's 1738 Map of Gvozdev's Voyage
redrawn from Golder

I Introduction

A. Everything Russian

Why is it that M.S. Gvozdev receives so little recognition for being the first European to discover America exploring from the west? L.A. Goldenberg writes, "the name Gvozdev is well known only in a small circle of scholars..."[1] Historians of this period from both sides of the Bering Strait have attempted to answer this question. William Hunt is a member of the American school which reasons that the first Russians to discover the American coast from the west did not gain full credit because they did not land.[2] A careful review of the record exposes an error in this line of reasoning.

The first recorded Russian landing on an Alaskan island was led by Peter Chaplin on St. Lawrence Island in August of 1728. C.L. Urness writes: "The Russians reached this island on August 10 and named it St. Lawrence Island. A boat was sent from the ship to the island, where houses were found, but no people were seen."[3] In Bering's report, he says that he sent Chaplin to the island twice in search of people.[4]

The first Russian landing on the Alaskan mainland was led by Pushkarev on the Alaska Peninsula in 1761.[5] Chaplin and Pushkarev have received even less recognition than that of Gvozdev. What, then, is the relationship between "landing" and "recognition" as it relates to the Russian discovery of Alaska?

Others attribute the scarcity of recognition for the discovery to the failure of the expedition to discover anything of commercial value.[6] This belief, however, is inconsistent with the extant reports about the expedition recounted independently by two of its participants. In a sworn statement dated April 10, 1741, found in the files of G.F. Muller, Skurikhin, a member of Gvozdev's crew, reported the expedition returning from Alaska with marten parkas, cross fox pelts and red fox pelts and the existence of large forests of larch, spruce and popular and many reindeer.[7] Gvozdev's account dated September 9, 1741, refers to coniferous trees, reindeer, marten, fox and beaver in the Big Land as well.[8]

Still others assert that Gvozdev did not have a much better appreciation of exactly what he saw in 1732 than did Columbus on another voyage 240 years earlier.[9] Even if this contention were correct it would not nullify the significance of either discovery. Yet the record shows that Gvozdev was: 1) ordered to sail the *St. Gabriel* to the Big Land, 2) the members of the expedition recognized what they saw as being the Big Land and 3) Gvozdev thought the Big Land was part of America.

1) "..so Pavlutski ordered Fedorov and Gvozdev to go on Bering's ship, the *Sviatoi Gavriil*, to look for the Big Land."[10] 2) In the sworn statement found in G.F. Muller's files mentioned above, Skurikhin reports the following concerning their approach to the shore of Alaska: "When they were within half a verst of it they realized it was not an island, but a large land with a coast of yellow sand."[11] 3) Lomonosov writes: "What is the land opposite Cape Chukchi - island or continent? The well-known geodesist Gvozdev believes, and the natives declare irrefutably, that all of it belongs to America."[12]

Russian historian, Raisa V. Makarova, also discusses attitudes towards Gvozdev's discovery in her introduction to *Russians in the Pacific 1743-1799* where she writes:

"The well known American Historian Frank Golder also displayed great interest in the former Russian possessions in the Western hemisphere. However, in his *Russian Expansion on the Pacific* and *Bering's Voyages*, Golder writes negatively on the Russian movement to the Pacific and of the Russian discoveries. Moreover, he stubbornly maintains that S. Dezhnev did not make his historic voyage and did not discover the strait separating Asia and America. Suffice it to say that this assertion has been refuted by his American colleagues. Golder displayed similar tendentiousness in relation to other moments in the history of Russian exploration on the Pacific, as for example, in his evaluation of the results of the expedition of I. Fedorov and M. Gvozdev. His generally negative conception of the character and importance of Russian geographic discoveries, and his desire to minimize or even deny them altogether is characteristic of a whole group of foreign scholars."[13]

Did Golder write tendentiously regarding the expedition of Fedorov and Gvozdev? Have a whole group of foreign scholars attempted to minimize the importance of the Russian discovery of Alaska? If Makarova's assertions are correct, it would certainly explain why Gvozdev has received little recognition for his discovery. Equally important is the basis of these foreign scholars' reports. To this end, the reporting of Gvozdev's voyage that came out of Russia during the first century after the discovery will be presented, followed by a summary of subsequent reports by English and American historians.

Of the four reports presented below, only one was official. The first report came in the form of a French newspaper article that was based upon an interview on March 1, 1738 with F.I. Soimonov, then Governor of Siberia:

"The Captain-commander Beerings on his return from his first voyage met ten sailors who were sent to the Eastern Ocean. They went on board the boat left by Captain Beerings and, following his route, then went to Kamchatka and even beyond that where they discovered two gulfs A, B. From there they steered east and found the island C and a large body of land D, a half days distance from the land F. While they were near this land there came to them a man in a small boat similar to those of Greenland. He was asked what country that was and whether there were any fur-bearing animals, but he could not give them any information. For two days they sailed along coast D E of this country going in a southerly direction. They attempted to make a landing but a storm forced them back to Kamchatka. They cruised along among the islands at the southern part of Kamchatka and came as far as the large island opposite the mouth of the Amur River. They landed on the island and found among the Tartars, who inhabited this place, three Russian captives. Taking them along they sailed for the Eastern Ocean, north of the Amur River, and finally to Okhotsk. The Russian pilot, who was engaged in this navigation for two consecutive summers, died, and he was succeeded by a German who, with his journal and sailors, came to Tobolsk. They got into a fight and one of the sailors was sent from Tobolsk to St. Petersburg for trial, and, when questioned, he gave the information just mentioned. The Admiralty College wishing to know more about this discovery sent an order to Tobolsk (only a few days ago) that the German with the journal and all others connected with this voyage should come to the capital. Mr. Soimonof said that it is hard to understand why Captain Beerings, who in his first voyage in the waters south of Kamchatka - from Bolshaja Reka to Kamchatka Gulf, made no mention of these islands south of Kamchatka; it would seem that, according to the report of Captain Spanberg, who was over the same waters as Captain Beerings, that these islands may be seen from Kamchatka and that the inhabitants even pay tribute to His Imperial Majesty."[14]

The map on page vi accompanied this newspaper article.

The second published report of the discovery of Alaska came from Russia by way of France as well. J.N. Delisle published it in Paris in 1752 with the map on page 6.

"On the coast of the Eastern Sea, over against Kamchatka, is a place called Okhota or Okhoskoy-ostrog, in the latitude of 59 degrees, and 22 minutes, and near 141 degrees longitude distance from the meridian of Paris. This is the place for taking shipping for Kamchatka and the neighboring countries; and Mr. Beerings having here left the ship in which he made his first voyage, some Russians ventured to put to sea with it, in 1731, steering the same course as Mr. Beerings had done two years before, but with better success than him, having carried the discovery of a way to America farther than he, for reaching the point whither Captain Beerings had gone in his first voyage, and which had his *ne plus ultra*, that stood directly eastward, where they met with an island and afterwards a large country, which they had not been long in sight of, before a man in a little skiff, like those of the Greenlanders, came

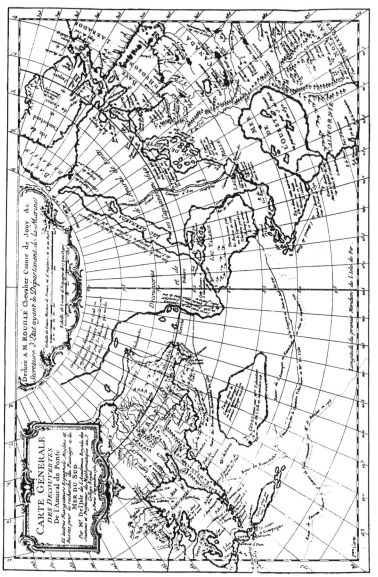

Delisle's map published in 1752

up to them. They were very desirous of knowing what country it was he belonged to, but all they could gather from him was, that he lived in a very large continent, which abounded with furs. The Russians traced the coast of this continent two days in a south direction, without being able to land, when they met with such a storm as obliged them to bear away for the coast of Kamchatka, returning afterwards to the place from whence they had set out."[15]

The third published report on the discovery of Alaska came from G.F. Muller, the official historian of Russia, via Germany in 1753. It was part of the unofficial Russian response to the Delisle report above. It is entitled *A Letter from a Russian Naval Officer.* Muller writes:

"Mr. Delisle mentions another discovery made by the Russians, who in the year 1731, ventured to take the same course that Mr. Beerings had taken two years before in his first voyage. Here it is to be observed, that in the year 1730, Mr. Pawlutski, at the time Captain of foot, and one Shestakov, chief of the Cossacks of Yakouzk, were appointed to reduce the Tschuktschi, a wild refractory people, who had revolted against out court; and in order to have in readiness all necessaries for the army's subsistence, Mr. Pawlutski sent Mr. Gwosdew the surveyor, to find out those provisions, which where remaining of Mr. Beerings first expedition, with instructions to bring them to Tschuktschi, in the vessel left by Mr. Beerings in Ochozk.

Gwosdew acquitted himself perfectly well of his commission, bringing his vessel to Serzecaman, without the least mischance; but here he neither found Mr.

To the American Coast

Pawluski nor could he get any tidings of him, which obliged him to put back for Ochozk; but here, though he had no thought of making new discoveries, he was carried by the wind on the coast of America, opposite to the land of Tschuktschi, and at no great distance from it. I have never heard that he got sight of anyone of the natives of that country, which renders very doubtful that narrative of Mr. Delisle, about a conversation held between the captain and the Americans, and between people too, who couldn't understand one another's language."[16]

The central portion of Muller's map of 1754-1758 is presented on the next page.

The fourth published report was Russia's official report of the discovery of Alaska. It came directly from G.F. Muller in 1758, the official historian of Russia, as part of volume III of *Sammlung russischer geschichte*.

"Three days before this unfortunate event Shestakov had sent an order to Tauisk ostrog, directing the Cossack Trifon Krupischev to go to Bolsheretsk ostrog in a sea worthy vessel, from there to sail around the southern tip of Kamchatka and put in at Nizhne-Kamchatsk ostrog. Furthermore, he was to continue his voyage in the same vessel until he reached the Anadyr River and then invite the inhabitants of the large land lying opposite to pay tribute to Russia. If the geodesist Gvozdev wanted to accompany them, Krupischev was to take him on the vessel and show him all good will. There is no information about what happened afterwards. We only know that in 1730 the geodesist Gvozdev actually was on a foreign coast not far from the Chukchi's land. It is also known

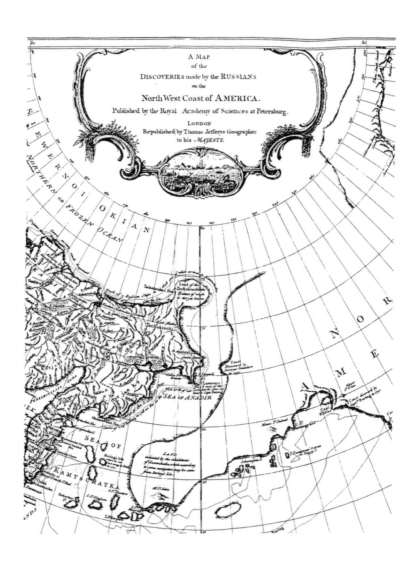

Portion of Muller's Map of 1754-1758

9

that Gvozdev found people with whom he could not speak for lack of a translator.

While this happened, the nobleman Ivan Shestakov had sailed to Kamchatka in the ship *Gabriel* and reached Bolsheretsk on 19 September 1729. Although he had been ordered to go to Uda River, that was impossible because of an adverse, severe storm. The following summer he made the voyage to Uda, came to Uda ostrog, and found the people who had been sent there by Chief Shestakov, who had built a useless ship. Shestakov then sailed back toward Kamchatka, seeing various islands both in route out and back, and finally returned to Okhotsk. I regret that I cannot present the circumstances of this voyage. In a report which the nobleman Shestakov submitted to the chancellery at Iakutsk on 23 October 1730, however, the days on which the various events are noted; we will add these as proof.

16 June	1730	Departure from the Bolshaia River
16 July	"	Arrival at the Uda River
19 July	"	Arrival at Uda ostrog
28 July	"	Departure from there
13 August	"	Arrival at Bolshaia River
20 August	"	Departure from there
5 September	"	Arrival at Okhotsk

Just at the time Shestakov came back to Okhotsk, the navigator Jacob Gens received an order from Captain Pavlutski, who had meanwhile come from Irkutsk to Nizhne-Kolymsk zimovye, or ostrog, by the usual land route. The order stated that although Pavlutski had received word from Anadyr ostrog of the Cossack chief Shestakov's death, the expedition would continue without hindrance. The navigator Gens should round Kamchatka to Anadyrsk in one of the vessels Captain Bering left behind at

Okhotsk. Captain Pavlutski would also set out for Anadyrsk shortly afterwards, etc.

Following his orders, Gens took the ship *Gabriel* and sailed to Kamchatka. On July 20, 1731 he stood at the mouth of the Kamchatka River, preparing to continue his voyage to Anadyr River, when the report was delivered to him that a rebellious mob of Kamchadals had gone to Nizhne-Kamchatsk ostrog on the same day, killed most of the Russians there, and set fire to the houses of the inhabitants. The few surviving Russians took refuse in their vessel. Gens sent some men to bring the Kamchadals under control again, which then followed. Thus the sea voyage to Anadyr was left undone."[17]

The information presented in the first report of 1738 is out of order. It refers, almost at random, to events scattered over an eight year period. One would have to be very familiar with all the details surrounding the discovery in order to understand the article. The second article, published in 1752, has the basic information correct while several of the details are in error. Unfortunately, the third report, purportedly coming from a Russian Naval Officer, was supposed to correct the errors in the French report of 1752 but instead erroneously presents the discovery as if it happened by accident. The fourth report, the only official Russian report on the discovery of Alaska, is so scrambled that it is described by an American historian of this period as "cryptic and puzzling" in a 1992 publication.[18]

Let us now take a look at how English and American historians have dealt with these reports during the two centuries following their publication. It may be noted that the use of the year 1730 invariably has Muller as its source, 1731 has Delisle as its source and the use of 1732 indicates some familiarity with Gvozdev's reports.

1761 In 1761 and again in 1764, T. Jefferys published *Voyages from Asia to America*, English translations of Muller's 1758 publication mentioned above.

1777 William Robertson, in *History of America*, addresses the report(s) of the location of the American continent relative to Asia with a great deal of skepticism. He, at a minimum, has Muller's report of 1758 as his footnote "n" below indicates and he probably has the map that accompanied it as well.

After discussing Bering and Chirikov's voyages, he writes, "It is probable the future navigators in those seas, by steering farther to the north, may find that the continent of America approaches still nearer to Asia. According to the barbarous people, who inhabit the country about the north-east promontory of Asia, there lies off the coast, a small island, to which they sail in less than a day. From that, they can descry a large continent, which, according to their description, is covered with forests, and possessed by people whose language they do not understand[n]. By them they are supplied with the skins of martens, an animal unknown in the northern parts of Siberia, and which is never found but in countries abounding with trees. If we could rely on this account, we might conclude, that the American continent is separated from ours only by a narrow strait, and all the difficulties with respect to the communication between them would vanish. Perhaps the merit of ascertaining this is reserved for the sovereign now seated on the throne of Peter the Great, who, by perfecting his plan may add this splendid event to those which already distinguish her reign."[19]

As one of the first commentaries by a leading foreign historian reporting on the discovery of Alaska after the official Russian account was published, it gives us some insight as to how other historians may have viewed Muller's report. Observe that Robertson was very familiar with Muller's report of 1758 as he refers to pages 4, 5, 141, 148, 166, 248, 249, 267, and 276 which includes the two sentences about Gvozdev's discovery. Footnote "n" above refers to Muller's second sentence on the discovery.

Robertson's initial source of reference is not to Muller's or Gvozdev's reports but of "the barbarous people, who inhabit the country about the north-east promontory of Asia." Robertson casts doubt on the veracity of "this account" but speculates that "the American continent is separated from ours only by a narrow strait." Then he suggests that the Czarist might send an expedition there to see if he is correct.

It would appear that Robertson either did not understand Muller's account or did not believe it.

1780 & 1787 Although Wlliam Coxe did not mention the Russian discovery of Alaska in his 1780 work entitled *Account of the Russian Discoveries between Asia and America*, his appendix VII does discuss reports about the location of America "drawn from a barbarour people" similar to Robertson's above. In his 1787 publication entitled *A Comparative View of the Russian Discoveries with those made by Captains Cook and Clerke,* Coxe writes, "That promontory lying opposite to the country of the Tchutski, which, according to Muller, was first seen by Gvozdef in 1730, and the most western point of which is represented on the chart that accompanies his Russian discoveries.."[20]

While in Russia in 1778, Coxe discussed Russian discoveries with various scholars there including G.F. Muller. Muller's copy of Skurikhin's one thousand word sworn statement about Gvozdev's voyage to Alaska in 1732 was apparently not among the things they discussed.

1819 Another English author to write on the subject was Captain James Burney who quotes both Muller's 1753 story using 1730 as the date of the discovery and Delisle's 1752 story using the date of 1731. In his book, Burney makes it sound as if Gvozdev sailed to America twice.[21] In so doing, Burney reports the initial discovery as an accident.

1870 In 1870 American author William H. Dall published *Alaska and Its Resources.* Dall also tries to accommodate both Delisle and Muller by writing that in a boat constructed out of the wreckage of the *Fortuna*, Gwosdeff reached Anadyrsk in September of 1730. In the spring of 1731 he was driven east-ward by a gale and found the shores of America.[22] The "gale" to which Dall refers comes straight out of Muller's *A Letter*. The implication here again is that discovery was happenstance, as in Muller's report of 1753.

1886 Bancroft published his *History of Alaska* in San Francisco. In it he describes the Russian discovery of Alaska as follows: "After battling with adverse winds and misfortunes for about two years, the explorers passed northward along the Asiatic shore, by the gulf of Anadir, noting the Diomede Islands, and perhaps catching a glimpse of the American shore."[23] *Adverse winds?* Bancroft simply reported what Muller published in *A Letter from a Russian Naval Officer.*

Bancroft goes on to quote Muller, believing that he is quoting Gvozdev. "On their return to Kamchatka," he writes, "they made the most contradictory statements before the authorities. From Gvozdef's report we are told that at some time during the year 1730 he found himself between latitude 65^0 and 66^0, 'on a strange coast, situated opposite, at a small distance from the country of Chukchi, and that he found people there, but could not speak with them for want of an interpreter.'"[24] *Contradictory statements? Gvozdev "found himself on a strange coast"?* Bancroft doesn't understand Muller's reports.

Bancroft's footnote for this quote indicates that he senses a problem of some kind. Before summarizing Gvozdev's report, he writes, "It is possible that Gvozdef's voyage was of greater importance than the writers of that period ascribed to it."

Later, as part of his account of Chirikov off the Alaskan coast in 1741, Bancroft writes, " But even Chirikof, who amongst Russians was the noblest and most chivalrous of them all, if we may believe the story of Gvozdef, may not justly set up the claim as first discoverer of northwester-most America. True, Gvozdef saw only what anyone might see if sailing through the strait of Bering -- he says he saw or found himself on the land opposite Asia."[25]

Note that Gvozdev did not say that "he found himself on the land opposite Asia," Muller implies this in his report of 1753 when he writes, "he was carried by the wind on the coast of America, opposite to the land of Tschuktschi.." Gvozdev reported that he sailed east from

15

the Chukchi cape and the Diomede Islands in search of the "Big Land."

1906 The Government Printing Office Published Marcus Baker's *Geographic Dictionary of Alaska* in 1906. Baker writes, "Michael Gvozdev, surveyor, also explored the Bering Strait, in 1730, and after him the islands have been called by the Russians Gvozdef Islands."[26] Using the date of 1730, Baker show familiarity with Muller's report(s) and not Gvozdev's.

1910 Clarke uses Delisle's date of 1931 and refers to Gvozdev as an adventurer in a one-half sentence report of the discovery.[27]

1912 Edward Heawood describes the discovery as follows: "At the same time a voyage seems to have been made independently, under his (Afanacy Shestakov's) orders, and in it Gvozdef apparently took part, for it is recorded that in 1730 he reached a land opposite the Chukche country in $65^066'$N., which must, it seems, have been the American continent."[28] Note the use of Muller's phrase "a land opposite the Chukche country" and year of 1730. Heawood concludes the paragraph evaluating the geographic results of the Shestakov-Pavlutski Expedition as "by no means striking."[29] The only familiarity that Heawood seems to have about the discovery is that of Muller's reports.

1914 Frank Golder, in his *Russian Expansion on the Pacific, 1641-1850* in 1914 and volume one of *Bering's Voyages* in 1922, quotes most of Gvozdev's report of the voyage but adds the following footnote in both volumes,

"In the *Lettre d'un officier de la marine ressienne,* 1753 (see bibliography), the statement is made that Pavlutski ordered Gvozdev to bring the provisions left by Bering to the country of the Chukchi, whom Pavlutski was fighting. Gvozdev could not find Pavlutski and started back and accidentally ran into the American coast."[30]

1931 J.N.L. Baker, without mentioning Gvozdev by name, offers the following one sentence report on the discovery of Alaska. "It is probable that the Russians saw part of the American continent in 1732, though they were unaware of this fact, and it was not until 1741 that they had definite knowledge of the New World."[31] Baker, and Brebner below, are two examples that Makarova noted as being among those historians who attempt to minimize the significance of Russian discoveries.

1933 Brebner, also without mentioning Gvozdev by name writes, "a sea expedition incidental to a war against the natives of the North-East, happened on America in the summer of 1732 and mapped part of the coast without being aware of the achievement."[32]

1970 238 years after the Russian discovery of Alaska, C.C. Hulley, head of the department of History and Political Science at the University of Alaska in Fairbanks from 1945 to 1955, concludes his chapter on the discovery of Alaska in his third edition of *Alaska: Past and Present* as follows:

"At this point it might be appropriate to say that there are those who maintain the Chirikof and Bering were not the first white men to see Alaska's coasts. There are tales

17

about other Russians who are reported to have seen the North American continent from Siberia before 1741. The authenticity of all these tales is open to question....In 1732, the geodesist, Michael Gvozdef, a member of the Shestakov expedition, is reported to have seen a large land mass to the east while reconnoitering the eastern coast of Siberia..."[33]

Is Raisa Makarova correct when she asserts that Golder and other historians attempt to minimize or deny imporant Russian discoveries such as the discovery of Alaska? The record reveals that she is. What is the basis of these reports? Almost inevitably the source is G.F. Muller's account of 1753 in which he implies that the discovery was nothing more than an accident or the writer does not understand the report(s), including the one of 1758, or perhaps does not believe them. For years Muller was accused of either withholding information about Russian discoveries or publishing misleading reports about them.

Muller made two reports of the Russian discovery of Alaska which may be summarized as follows:

1753 "...though he (Gvozdev) had no thought of making new discoveries, he was carried by the wind on the coast of America, opposite the land of the Tschuktschi, and at no great distance from it."[34]

1758 "We only know that in 1730 the geodesist Gvozdev actually was on a foreign coast not far from the Chukchi's land."[35]

No significant reports on the discovery came out of Russia for nearly a century after Muller's 1758 publication. Is it any wonder then, that Gvozdev receives so little recognition for his discovery of Alaska?

In *The Eskimos of the Bering Strait, 1650-1898*, Dorothy Ray writes: "Gvozdev's journey was overshadowed by Bering's Expedition, especially as related to the writings of Gerhard Muller, who lived in Yakutsk from 1735 until 1737. Although in 1758 Muller wrote a short paragraph concerning the Gvozdev discovery, it seems strange that he did not give it more attention since, as a leading historian, he presumably had access to the logbook of the *Gabriel,* Fedorov's journal (if there was one), and the Gvozdev-Spanberg maps."[36]

Leo Bagrow explains how Muller's reporting (see page iii above for Muller's standard) of an event such as Gvozdev's discovery could have been recorded in such a cavalier fashion. He writes, "Contention between the native-born Russian and the imported Western-European groups of Academicians lasted right through the whole 18th century, the foreign element decrying everything Russian."[37]

B. Further Clarification

In a 1982 article entitled, "The 250th Anniversary of the Discovery of Alaska," B.P. Polenoy writes: "But one thing is clear: the world's geographers first heard of the existence of Alaska from Russian sources. And so the honor of the discovery of Alaska unquestionably belongs to Russian pathfinders." He also notes the "the history of the discovery of Alaska by the Russians still needs further clarification."[38] This section is an attempt to clarify the reports of the discovery that came out of Russia during the eighteenth century.

To the American Coast

F.I. Soimonov

As noted above, the basis of the first published account of the Russian discovery of Alaska was an interview on March 1, 1738 by a French journalist with F.I. Soimonov, Governor of Siberia. About this interview Goldenberg writes:

"This interview with Soimonov was apparently based on verbal information from Bering himself and not Gvozdev's report. The article was never published in the Russian language.

During the interview Soimonov said that the 'Big Land' was a half day by sea from the Northeastern end of Asia. Published in the same newspaper was a good map of the route of the voyage of Fedorov and Gvozdev drawn by J.N. Delisle from Soimonov's report. One of the inaccuracies of this first cartographic publication about the first successful voyage to the coast of America from the Russian side was the lack of King Island (Ukivok) and the representation of only one, not two Diomede Islands.

Soimonov's report is associated with the discussion of the Admiralty College of February 12 and 14, 1738 about the Fedorov-Gvozdev Expedition. At that time there was no accurate information because of the lack of a complete report. This explains the fragmentary and inaccurate nature of the F.I. Soimonov interview. It was only later that it became known that the members of the sea portion of the expedition of Captain D.I. Pavlutski and Yakut Cossack leader A.P. Shestakov, assistant Navigator Fedorov and geodesist M.S. Gvozdev made a remarkable voyage in 1732 on the *St. Gabriel* which concluded in the discovery of the northwestern coast of America and first landing on Ratmanov Island."[39]

The title of the article is, "Navigation and Discoveries made by Russians in the Eastern (Pacific) Ocean between the Two Voyages of Captain Beerings During the Years 1731 and 1732." The subtitle is: "New Information Regarding Eastern Lands Furnished by Mr. Fedor Ivanitch Soimonof, March 1, 1738."[40]

The capital letters in the article refer to the map of J.N. Delisle (see page vi above) published with the article. The numbers to the left of the sentences of the article are mine and represent the order in which the events actually occurred.

1. The Captain-commander Beerings on his return from his first voyage met ten sailors who were sent to the Eastern Ocean.

5. They went on board the boat left by Captain Beerings and, following his route, then went to Kamchatka and beyond that where they discovered two gulfs A, B.

6. From there they steered east and found the island C and a large body of land D, a half days distance from the land F.

9. While they were near this island there came to them a man in a small boat similar to those of Greenland.

10. He was asked what country that was and

whether there were any fur-bearing animals,
but he could not give them any satisfactory
information

7. For two days they sailed along coast D E of this
   country going in a southerly direction.

8. They attempted to make a landing but a storm
   came up forcing them back to Kamchatka.

2. They cruised among the islands at the southern
   part of Kamchatka and came as far as the large
   island opposite the mouth of the river Amur.

3. They landed on the island and found among the
   Tartar, who inhabit this place, three Russian
   captives.

4. Taking them along they sailed for the Eastern
   Ocean, north of the Amur River, and finally to
   Okhotsk.

11. The Russian pilot, who was engaged in this nav-
    gation for two consecutive summers, died, and
    he was succeeded by a German, with his journal
    and sailors, came to Tobolsk.

12. They got into a fight and one of the sailors was
    sent from Tobolsk to St. Petersburg for trial, and,
    when questioned, he gave the information just
    mentioned.

13. The Admiralty College, wishing to know more

about this discovery sent an order to Tobolsk (only a few days ago) that the German with his journal and all others connected with this voyage should come to the capital.

14. Mr. Soimonof said that it is hard to understand why Captain Beerings, who in his first voyage sailed in the waters south of Kamchatka-from Bolshaja to Kamchatka Gulf, made no mention of these islands south of Kamchatka; it would seem that, according to the report of Captain Spanberg, who was over the same waters as Captain Beerings, that these islands may be seen from Kamchatka and that the inhabitants even pay tribute to His Imperial Majesty.[41]

Bering returned to Okhotsk from Kamchatka July 24, 1729 and left shortly thereafter for St. Petersburg. Bering met Shestakov's detachment (sentence #1) August 12, as Shestakov was en route to Okhotsk.[42]

Sentences 2, 3 and 4 relate to the voyages of Ivan Shestakov, Afancy's nephew aboard the *St. Gabriel* and Vasilii Shestakov, Afancy's son aboard the *Fortune*[43] as shown in the lower portion of map of voyage on page vi. These voyages occurred during the last half of 1729 through the first part of September 1730. See a summary of Ivan Shestakov's travels aboard the *St. Gabriel* is found in paragraph 2 of Muller's report of 1758.

Sentences five through ten relate to the voyage of Fedorov and Gvozdev to Alaska in 1732, depicted in the upper right portion of the map above.

The Russian pilot in sentence 11 is Fedorov who died in Kamchatka in 1733. Fedorov was an assistant navigator. The German Gens, a navigator, went to Tobolsk.

The sailor who had been sent from Tobolsk to St. Petersburg in the twelfth sentence was Leonti Petrov,[44] a member of the Shestakov-Pavlutski Expedition. Petrov took part in the Gvozdev-Fedorov voyage to Alaska. He had made a false report in 1735 which led to the events described.[45]

The order issued in sentence thirteen was for the German (Gens) to come to the capital. But Gens died in 1737.[46]

The fourteenth sentence contains criticism of Bering's role in the First Kamchatka Expedition typical of that time.

J.N. Delisle

Joseph Nicolas Delisle, a French geographer and astronomer, accepted an invitation by the Russian Academy of Science to assist J.K. Kirlov who directed all the cartographic work for the Russian Senate. Delisle arrived in St. Petersburg in 1726. According to Breitfuss, he was suspected of secreting copies of Russian maps and memoirs back to France through his Embassy. While he was never caught, 300-350 such documents are now in Paris, "most having arrived there long ago."[47] Delisle retired from the Russian Academy in 1747 after 21 years of service and returned to Paris. On April 8, 1750 he presented to the

Paris Academy of Science a map of the North Pacific Ocean and a memorandum giving the most distorted explanation of new discoveries made in this area of the world. He published both the map and the report two years later.[48]

While the area of the map representing Alaska is virtually unrecognizable (see page 6 above), the portion of the memorandum about the Russian discovery is relatively accurate, though the date is wrong. A careful analysis of Delisle's report and sentences five through ten of the newspaper account from Soimonov in 1738 suggest that the latter is the former's primary source. Note the comparison of the kayak to those found in Greenland, the sailing along the coast for two days, and the mention of only one island in both narrations.

G.F. Muller, *A Letter,*

The third published report of the discovery of Alaska came from Muller via Germany. Gerhard Freidrich Muller came to Russia in 1725 at the age of twenty and became a student at the Academy of Science. He made acquaintance with Kirilov and Bering shortly thereafter and spent ten years in Siberia researching its history and geography[49] He became the official Russian historian of the day and is often called the Father of Siberian History.[50]

When Delisle published his account of Russian discoveries in the North Pacific (above), it was Muller who was called upon to respond. This response came in the form of an anonymous work entitled, *A Letter from a Russian Naval Officer,* published in 1753. As indicated above, this fanciful account makes the Russian discovery of Alaska sound like an accident.

It is not clear from where Muller obtained the date of 1730. It may have been from Waxell or perhaps from a map published in 1746 by the heirs of Homann that bore on the east shore of the Bering Strait, "Detecta a Gwosdew 1730."[51] Greely, Golder and Stejneger believed Lieutenant Waxell was the author of the article.[52] However, while Muller was in fact the author, the article was based upon the journal of Sven Waxell.[53]

Waxell had every reason to know that the information about Gvozdev in Muller's *A Letter* was incorrect. When M.S. Gvozdev presented his report to the Okhotsk chancellery April 13, 1741, about his voyage to America in 1732, Sven Waxell was present.[54] But Waxell, it seems, had a history of interesting renditions of events. For example, as second in command of Bering's voyage to America in 1741, "Waxell was convinced that he had 'spoken' to the Americans through the vocabulary included in a dubious travel account by Baron de Lahontan."[55] Even so, one could hardly blame Muller for going ahead and using Waxell's journal anyway. Muller's sources were somewhat limited because questions had been raised about his loyalty to Russia.[56]

Apparently Muller did eventually learn of the inaccuracy of his *A Letter*. Five years later when he was writing on the same subject he dropped the business about Gvozdev heading for Okhotsk from Anadyr and being carried by the wind to the coast of America. He also concurred with Delisle regarding his statement that members of the crew of the *St. Gabriel* tried to communicate with an American but were unable to do so. Muller also learned the correct date of 1732 for the Russian Discovery of Alaska. In Muller's files is the sworn statement of Ilia Skurikhin, a member of Gvozdev's crew, about the voyage dated April 10, 1741. Captain Shmalev witnessed this statement[57] and later sent a copy to Muller.[58] Muller had a lot of information about Gvozdev's discovery.

The map that Muller published about the same time as *A Letter* was as accurate as his account of the Russian discovery of Alaska was fanciful. Breitfuss writes, "Wonderfully accurate also is the position of Cape Gvozdev (now Cape Prince of Wales) and Mount Elias on Muller's map of 1754, for which the longitude of 210^0E., and 255^0E. respectively, from Ferro could have been obtained from Gvozdev (1732) and Bering (1741)... Here also it may be seen that the longitudes differ from the actual ones by only one degree. As regards the latitudes of these two points, they differ from the truth even less than that."[59]

Breitfuss is not the first to notice the accuracy in the location of the coast of Alaska in the Bering Strait on Muller's map. In 1781 Pallas wrote, "It is worthy of note that the coast of the American Continent opposite Chukchi Cape as delineated on our old maps on the basis of Gvozdev's discoveries precisely coincide, in terms of both latitude and longitude with that determined by Captain Cook."[60]

"In 1819 V.N. Berkh suggests that Gvozdev determined 'the latitudes of the three little islands in Bering Strait and the American cape lying opposite them with mathematical precision.'"[61] Yet today not even all Russian historians fully appreciate the accuracy of the Gvozdev map. In 1992, Amir A. Khisamutdinov, President of Far Eastern Studies Society in Vladivostok wrote of the distance across Bering Strait, "Presumably, the Gvozdev-Fedorov expedition failed to record such important information."[62] It is ironic that the map of geographer Delisle is as inaccurate as his account of the Russian discovery of Alaska is correct while just the opposite is true of historian Muller.

G.F. Muller's
Sammlung russischer geschichte, Vol. III

This is the only official Russian account of the Shestakov-Pavlutski Expedition and the two Bering Expeditions published in the eighteenth century. Four paragraphs of the section on the Shestakov-Pavlutski Expedition are Muller's description of the Russian discovery of Alaska. This account is so mixed up that an American historian of this period refers to it in a 1992 publication as "cryptic and puzzling."[63]

Goldenberg writes that Muller's "mistake was frequently repeated in Russian and foreign publications during the second half of the eighteenth century."[64] The key to understanding this portion of Muller is that the four paragraphs on the Russian discovery of Alaska are the five orders, or results thereof, given by the two leaders of the expedition, Shestakov and Pavlutski, to four subordinates over a period of two years and nine months to, among other things, sail the *St. Gabriel* to Alaska. For purposes of analysis, Muller's four paragraphs will be divided into five paragraphs; 1a, 1b, 2, 3 and 4 and then rearranged in the order in which the orders to sail to Alaska were given; 2, 1a, 3, 4 and 1b.

Order Number 1: Paragraph 2

"While this happened, the nobleman Ivan Shestakov had sailed to Kamchatka in the ship *Gabriel* and reached Bolsheretsk on 19 September 1729. Although he had been ordered to go to the Uda River, that was not possible because of an adverse, severe storm. The following summer he made the voyage to Uda, came to Uda ostrog, and found the people who had been sent there by Chief Shestakov, who had built a useless ship. Shestakov then sailed back toward Kamchatka, seeing various islands both on route and back, and finally returned to Okhotsk. I regret that I cannot present the circumstances of this voyage here for lack of a journal kept during the voyage. In a report which nobleman Shestakov submitted to the chancellery at Iakutsk on 23 October 1730, however, the days on which various events happened are noted; we will add these as proof.

16 June	1730	Departure from the Bolshaia River
16 July	"	Arrival at the Uda River
19 July	"	Arrival at Uda ostrog
28 July	"	Departure from there
13 August	"	Arrival at Bolshaia River
20 August	"	Departure from there
5 September	"	Arrival at Okhotsk"[65]

A portion of the objectives of the Shestakov-Pavlutski Expedition included the exploration and mapping the south coast of Siberia,[66] investigation of the Shantar and Kurile Islands and sail to Alaska. [67] To accomplish these objectives, Vasilii Shestakov "was to take cargo to Bolsherestsk and investigate the Kurile Islands"[68] aboard the *Fortune*. At Okhotsk, September 1, 1729,[69] By Afanacy Shestakov's order "Ivan Shestakov aboard the *St. Gabriel* was to sail to the mouth of the Uda River, examine the Shantar and Kurile Islands and, if time permitted, go to the Big Land."[70]

To the American Coast

As may be noted from the report submitted to the chancellery, only a portion of the objectives were accomplished at this time. The Uda ostrog was a strategic outpost in those days. Part of its purpose was to establish and maintain a presence on the frontier with China to bolster Russia's claim to the area....south to the Amur River.[71]

Order Number 2: Paragraph 1a

"Three days before this unfortunate event Shestakov had sent an order to Tauisk ostrog, directing the Cossack Trifon Krupischev to go to Bolsheretsk ostrog in a sea worthy vessel, from there to sail around the southern tip of Kamchatka and put in at Nizhe-Kamchatsk ostrog. Furthermore, he was to continue his voyage in the same vessel until he reached the Anadyr River and then invite the inhabitants of the large land lying opposite to pay tribute to Russia. If the geodesist Gvozdev wanted to accompany them, Krupischev was to take him on the vessel and show him all good will. There is no information about what happened afterwards."[72]

"Early in the fall of 1729 Shestakov with a company of ninety-three men set sail for Penjinsk Bay, but on account of head winds he was forced to land off Taui River and sent the boat back."[73] Shestakov had planned to build a fort at Penjinsk Bay, march overland to the Oliutora River and build another fort there and then proceed to Anadyr.

The *Lion*, under the command of piatidesiatnik Ivan Lebedev, [74] was to follow Shestakov, who was aboard the *Eastern Gabriel*, as backup in the event of trouble and then make winter quarters on the Tigil River.[75] The *Lion* was unable to keep its appointed rendezvous. They

30

wintered instead on the Iana River where the Koriaks attacked, burning the boat and killing all but five members of the crew.[76]

Shestakov remained at Tauisk ostrog until November 23.[77] He had appointed Cossack Trifron Krupischev and grenadier S. Selvanov to command the detachment there.[78] Shestakov, with a detachment of over a hundred men marched along the coast of the Okhotsk Sea to the west shore of Penjinsk Bay.

By the time he reached the north end of the bay, his forces had increased to one hundred fifty by Koriaks he had conquered along the way. On March 14, in a battle with an unknown number of Chukchi, Shestakov was killed.[79]

Three days before the battle Shestakov sent the above order to Krupischev in Tauisk. The order arrived in Tauisk simultaneously with word of Shestakov's death causing chaos which in turn paralyzed the detachment.[80] No voyage was undertaken.

Order Number three: Paragraph 3

"Just at the time Shestakov came back to Okhotsk, the navigator Jacob Gens received an order from Captain Pavlutski, who had meanwhile come from Irkutsk to Nizhne-Kolymsk zimovye, or ostrog, by the usual land route. The order stated that although Pavlutski had received word from Anadyr ostrog of the Cossack chief Shestakov's death, the expedition would continue without hindrance. The navigator Gens should round Kamchatka to Anadyrsk in one of the vessels Captain Bering left behind at Okhotsk. Captain Pavlutski would also set out for Anadyrsk shortly afterwards, etc."[81]

Pavlutski received word of Shestakov's death on April 25.[82] The next day he sent word to Gens to sail to Anadyr "to speed up the concentration of the members of expedition in the Anadyr region and in the mouth of the Anadyr River.[83] Also, he wanted Gens to "bring the artillery reserves from Okhotsk to Anadyr ostrog at once."[84]

Gens, who sided with Pavlutski in his dispute with Shestakov, was in Okhotsk when he received the order. Gens sent word to the detachment at Tauisk to sail on the *Eastern Gabriel* to Okhotsk.[85] The *Eastern Gabriel* left Tauisk on July 1 and entered the mouth of the Okhota River on July 6.[86] They waited there until September for the return of the *St. Gabriel*.

Ivan Shestakov aboard the *St. Gabriel* failed to find the Shantar Islands and returned to Okhotsk in September, 1730.[87] On September 19, Gens aboard the *St. Gabriel* and Fedorov aboard the *Eastern Gabriel* sailed from Okhotsk reaching Kamchatka on September 30. The *Eastern Gabriel* wrecked off the Kamchatka coast in a storm. The detachment then waited on Bolsheresk for directions from Captain Pavlutski.[88] It is my opinion that the reason that they waited in Bolsheresk for further instructions from Pavlutski rather than proceeding to Nizhe-Kamchatsk and Anadyr as directed was because the artillery reserves that Pavlutski requested were on the *Eastern Gabriel* when it wrecked. These artillery reserves are never mentioned again.

Order Number Four: Paragraph 4

"Following his orders, Gens took the ship *Gabriel* and sailed to Kamchatka. On July 20, 1731 he stood at the mouth of the Kamchatka River, preparing to continue his voyage to Anadyr River, when the report was delivered to him that a rebellious mob of Kamchadals had gone to Nizhe-Kamchatsk ostrog on the same day, killed most of the Russians there, and set fire to the houses of the inhabitants. The few surviving Russians took refuse in their vessel. Gens sent some men to bring the Kamchadals under control again, which then followed. Thus the sea voyage to Anadyr was left undone."[89]

"Despite the April 26, 1730 instructions to all those who had departed with Shestakov on the 'Okhotsk Road' (the navigator, assistant navigator, geodesist, apprentice, grenadiers, soldiers and servicemen) to proceed to Anadyr, 'no one was coming' according to the report of Pavlutski to Tobolsk seven month later." On October 9, the Captain sent new orders to Kamchatka, specifically ordering Ivan Shestakov to immediately take on the ship, Gens, Fedorov, Gvozdev, Speshnev, the sailors and the servicemen and to proceed to the mouth of the Anadyr River."[90]

The October orders from Pavlutski in Anadyr were received in Bolsheresk December 28. These orders emphasized "the importance of their arrival at the mouth of the Anadyr River in time for further 'exploration of the islands.'"[91]

Sailing from Bolsheresk the following June 23, the *St. Gabriel* reached the mouth of the Kamchatka River on July 9.[92] As planned, on July 20, 1731, the *St. Gabriel* sailed for Anadyr. However, they were stopped by contrary winds at the mouth of the river and dropped anchor. The opportunity for the voyage was missed and it was canceled.[93] The Kamchadals were waiting for the *St.*

Gabriel to leave attacked the Russians remaining at Nizhe-Kamchatsk as soon as the ship sailed. Gens played a key role in putting down this rebellion.[94]

Order Number Five: Paragraph 1b

"We only know that in 1730 the geodesist Gvozdev actually was on a foreign coast not far from the Chukchi's land. It is also known that Gvozdev found people with whom he could not speak for lack of a translator."[95]

On February 1, 1932, Captain Dmitrii Pavlutski sent new directions from Anadyr to the detachment in Kam-chatka relieving Gens of his leadership role. He was to transfer all servicemen, soldiers and supplies to geodesist M.S. Gvozdev.[96] In his statement to Captain Spanberg on September 1, 1743, Gvozdev recalled the order that he received from Pavlutski on May 1. "We were instructed together with the navigator and assistant navigator (i.e. Gvozdev, Gens and Fedorov) to sail on the vessel *Gavrill* around Kamchatski Nos to the mouth of the Anadyr, and opposite Anadyrski Nos, which is called the Big Land, to investigate the number of islands there and inhabitants, to search for new ones and to collect tribute of furs from those who have not paid before."[97]

On July 23, 1732, the *St. Gabriel* sailed north from Kamchatka with Gvozdev, assistant navigator Fedorov, seafarer Moshkov and a crew of 37. They landed five times on the Chukchi Peninsula,[98] twice on Big Diomede Island, and discovered Little Diomede Island and Fairway Rock. On August 21, almost exactly three years from the initial order to sail to the Big Land, the American main-land was sited.[99]

34

Nine years later, Cossack I.F. Skurikhin reported to the Okhotsk office, "and half a verst before reaching it (the land - L.G.), we made out that it was not an island, but the Big Land, the shore of yellow sand. There were dwellings of yurts along the shore and a lot of people walking along the land. The woods on this land were great: Larch, Spruce, Poplar and a great number of deer."[100] After discovering King Island on August 22, they returned to Kamchatka September 28.

Summary of orders given to sail to the "Big Land"

Para-graph	Order by/ Locale	Order to/ Locale	Ship	Date
2	A.Shestakov *Okhotsk*	I. Shestakov Okhotsk	*St. Gabriel*	Sept 1, 1729
1a	A.Shestakov Penjinsk Bay	T.Krupischev Tauisk ostrog	A sea worthy vessel	Mar 1, 1730
3	D.Pavlutski Nizhne-Kolymsk ostrog	J. Gens Okhotsk	One of Bering's Vessels	Apr 26,1730
4	D.Pavlutski Anadyr	I.Shestakov Bolsheresk	*St. Gabriel*	Oct 9, 1730
1b	D.Pavlutski Anadyr	M.Gvozdev Nizhne-Kamchatsk	*St. Gabriel*	Feb 11, 1732

To the American Coast

C. Changing Attitudes

    The final quarter of the twentieth century has witnessed some change in attitudes about Gvozdev's discovery. For example:

1975 Dorothy Ray refers to the discovery as "a remarkable event."[101]

1978 Y.M. Svet and S.G. Fedorova write: "... the northwestern tip of the North American continent should have been named in honor of the Russian geodesist, Mikhail Spiridonov Gvozdev, and not Cape Prince of Wales."[102]

1982 B.P. Polevoi refers to Gvozdev's findings as an "important geographical discovery."[103]

1983 L.A. Goldenberg refers to it as a "very important geographical discovery."[104]

1990 A.I. Alekseev refers to Gvozdev's achievement as a "singularly outstanding voyage."[105]

1992 K.A. Shopotov writes: "The year 1992 is the 260th anniversary of the Russian Discovery of Alaska. It is an event to be celebrated, and its leaders....remembered."[106]

1994 Holland refers to the event as an "important discovery."[107]

1995 Marvin Falk writes of Gvozdev "actually reaching North America nine years before Bering and Chirikov.[108]

Perhaps one day it will be as Dorothy Ray suggests and Gvozdev will share in the credit for the Russian discovery of Alaska.[109]

> In spite of the Russian Columbus'
> predicted gloomy fate,
> they will discover a new way to the East
> between the icebergs,
> and our country will reach to America.[1]

These poetic and deeply patriotic words of genius Lomonosov express the belief that the Russian people would make their way from the Arctic Ocean to the Pacific.

At the same time, Lomonosov acknowledged the heroic feat of Columbus who crossed the Atlantic in 1492. Being sent in three ships by the government of Spain in search of "the Indies," e.g. East and South Asia, he landed on the Southern Baham Island on October 12. This day became the day of the discovery of America. During the next three expeditions (September 1493-June 1496, May 1498-November 1500, 1502-1504) Columbus discovered many of the islands of the West Indies in addition to the coasts of South and Central America.

The voyages of the fearless Columbus were very important. The 450th anniversary of his death will be on May 20, 1956. He was the first European to cross the Atlantic Ocean and make his way to the continent.

After Columbus, Spanish, Portuguese and other Western European explorers headed for the New World. They made discoveries about the nature of America and the people living there. It wasn't long before courageous explorers began to probe both American coasts.

We should not forget that these great geographical discoveries brought about colonization. By fire and sword

To the American Coast

Western Europeans turned native Americans into slaves
and destroyed their culture.

Indian tribes living on the American continents long
before Columbus created their "own science, art, and
spiritual life that still impress the entire world of culture.
The Inca and Mayan civilizations were well developed
when places like France, England and Germany were forests. The senseless destruction of their beautiful cultures,
the destruction and theft of their historic monuments and
treasures of art by ignorant European colonizers was one
of the most tragic events in the cultural history of man-
kind,"[2] writes W. Forster.

The discovery of America and a sea route to India and
the Far East around Africa stimulated the development of
capitalistic production in Europe and initiated the forma-
tion of the world market.

The Spanish, Portuguese, French, British, Italian and
Dutch people all contributed to the exploration of America. They marked their discoveries and the territories they
explored on maps. However, the completion of the entire
map of the continent became possible only after the discovery of Northwest America by Russian sailors. A significant portion of this achievement belongs of Gvozdev.

Forty-three years of the life of the famous geodesist
and explorer Mikhail Spiridonovich Gvozdev were spent
in the fleet in the Far East and in the development of Siberia. On the map of the Northwest American coast, discovered and explored by Gvozdev and Fedorov, is the
note: "Gvozdev was here in 1732." That note was retained
on later maps of the Northeastern portion of the Pacific
Ocean. One of the Diomede Islands was named after him.

The discovery of Northwest America by Russian sailors is a glorious page in the history of the exploration of

the world. Gvozdev's feat has been greatly appreciated in works of Russian and foreign scientists. In 1922, in his book about Bering's expeditions, famous American historian, F. Golder, who had worked in Russian archives, published Gvozdev's report of his voyage to the American coast.[3] L. Breitfuss, in his article, "Early Maps of Northeastern Asia," wrote that the expedition of Gvozdev and mariner Fedorov was a great event in the history of cartography.[4]

The discovery by Gvozdev and Fedorov was the anticipated result of many efforts of the Russian people. They had been trying to reach the coast of the Big Land since the middle of the seventeenth century in spite of many difficulties and shortages,

In 1648, Yakutian Cossack Semen Dezhnev and his crew, sailing from the mouth of the Kolya River, traveled along Northeastern Asia and then through the strait separating America and Asia. They sailed from the "Icy Sea" into the Pacific Ocean. Thanks to this voyage it was demonstrated that America was a separate continent. Some of his boats went to Alaska.

After the historic voyage of Semen Dezhnev, Russians tried several times to cross Bering Strait and reach the coast of the Big Land. After the founding of Anadyr ostrog in 1649, industrious people, as historian Polonski reports, went from Kolyma and Anadyr's ostrog by sea and land to Northeastern Chukotka to collect tribute to the Czar from people living there. Russians did not limit themselves to known regions, "but tried to cross the Anian Strait to the Big Land, known from Chukchi stories as the land which is rich with forests and animals, and populated by people who wore expensive sable and beaver coats."[5]

To the American Coast

Interest in Northwestern America increased in the beginning of the eighteenth century. In 1701, Atlasov, the famous explorer and discoverer of Kamchatka, reported "a cape between Kolyma and Anadyr" upon his arrival in Moscow. He said there was a cape "which goes to the sea (Chukchi Sea) and on the left side of the cape there is ice. During the winter the sea is frozen, and on the other side of that cape (Bering Sea), there is ice during spring and no ice during summer."

Atlasov was on the Chukchi Peninsula. His story is based upon information received from the native people. "And native people, the Chukchi who lived near the cape and the mouth of the Anadyr river, told the traveler that adjacent to the cape there is an island and, when the water is frozen during the winter, foreigners come from that island."[6]

The information Atlasov gives about the ice of the Chukchi Sea and Bering Strait is interesting. It proves that Russian explorers, after reaching the Far East, did not limit themselves to the research of specific regions but tried to gather as much information as possible.

In 1711 Peter Ilyich Popov, a Cossack from Yakutsk and a trader named Egor Vasilyevich Toldin lived on Cape Anadyr (Cape Dezhnev). According to the stories of the native people, they came to believe that a strait existed between Asia and America. They said that there were islands in the strait and that Chukchi were known to travel to them.

Five years later Colonel Elchinko received orders to go to the islands located adjacent to Cape Chukchi and explore them. However, the organization of the venture did not materialize.

In 1716 seamen Nagibin and Kuzakov traveled to the Arctic Ocean to find the island. While the voyage was not successful, the seamen were not discouraged. In 1720 Nagibin requested 200 men and ships "to explore the land located adjacent to the Chukchi islands." In his attempt to interest the government in the project, he said that "there were many animals there and people who could pay tribute."

Accordingly, based upon these various pieces of information, many Russians became convinced that there was a strait between Asia and America. But the width of the strait and the nature of the coast of the Big Land were not known. The information from Russian and native peoples about the Big Land required research. In his report to the Czar in 1713, Peter Saltykov said that he was certain one could travel from the Arctic Ocean to China, Japan and India. From his report, the idea of a separation between Asia and America spread throughout Russia.

The question as to whether Asia and America were connected excited many Western European scientists. This problem held the center of the attention of the famous German scientist Leybnits. In 1697 he sent a note through Hanover to the Russian embassy. In it he listed a number of questions by which he tried to attract the interest of the Russian Czar.[7]

Leybnits tried to keep abreast of all of the information regarding scientific and Arctic Ocean research by the Russian government. He believed that any success in this area would lead science to a positive solution to the discussion about a strait between Asia and America. That is why in 1711, in his letter to Admiral Bruce, Leybnits asked that he might be kept informed about the results of Russian activities in Siberia and the Arctic Ocean. In his letters he returned again and again to the scientific problem and expressed his hopes in Peter the Great who he saw as a great supporter of science and one who understood and supported scientific inquiry. "No one," wrote Leybnits, "can solve this problem better than the Czar. Its solution would be more glorious and important than anything done by the Egyptian Pharaohs in search of the sources of the Nile."[8]

In a note to Bruce dated September 23, 1712, Leybnits discussed the scientific programs in the field of magnetic and linguistic research in Russia. At the end of his note he mentioned the border between Asia and America. "In only one place," he wrote, "has the border not been sufficiently studied; and that place was governed by the Czar." Then he wrote about the big strip of land that goes north into the Arctic Ocean. He offered to explore it to determine "if there is a cape and if the strip of land ends there. I think the native people could make a voyage there during the summer. If not all at once then by using camps and slowly moving farther and farther." In Leybnits opinion, such exploration could be done not only by land but also by sea which would be much easier to accomplish. In the latter case, it would be possible to determine "if the land was becoming wider or narrower and hence the probability that there is a cape will increase or decrease. Sea currents, fish species and other conditions on both coasts will give us an opportunity to judge if the seas connect."[9] In a letter to the Czar from Vienna dated October 26, 1713, Leybnits again mentions the project.

In 1716, in Braunschweig, Leybnits met with Peter the Great on Piedmont's waters for about two weeks. During this meeting they undoubtedly discussed the question that Leybnits had been working on for 20 years. In a letter to

Bruce dated July 2, 1716, the German philosopher wrote that during their conversations, the Czar was interested in the mechanical sciences, "but his main interest concentrated on everything about sailing, and that is why he likes astronomy and geography. I hope that he will learn if Asia is connected to America." Leybnits underlined that idea in his letter dated June 22, 1716 to Shafirov in St. Petersburg.[10] In 1716 the Paris Academy of Science offered to Peter the Great to organize an expedition of French scientists to Northeast Russia and "through the people sent, find out if Siberia is connected to America."[11]

All of this indicates that in the beginning of the eighteenth century scientists wanted to find a solution to this important scientific question. The great discovery of Semen Dezhnev was not known in the West and was probably forgotten in Russia by this time.

In the list of the many Russian geographical discoveries in the northern portion of the Pacific Ocean during the seventeenth and eighteenth centuries, the foremost event is the voyage of Fedorov and Gvozdev to the coast of the Big Land.

In spite of the great scientific achievements of Gvozdev, limited sources prevent study and description of his life and work. The bibliography about the great researcher of the Far East and discoverer of Northwestern America is limited to a few special articles.[12] However, the list of those writing of his accomplishments is quite large.[13]

The geographical discoveries made by Russian sailors in the eighteenth century answered many scientific questions. The most important among these was the relationship between Asia and America. They discovered that the two continents are separated. The achievements of the Russian people are bright spots on the pages of the history of geographical discoveries. As a result, when the U.S. government decided to organize a Columbus exhibit in Chicago in 1892, they sought to have the "successful attempts of the Russian government to discover Alaska represented by the original report of Captain Vitus Bering of his voyages from 1728 to 1742. The discovery of Alaska occurred during this period."[14]

But other documents, in various archives, offer the possibility of learning more about the activities of the first discoverer.

Of most scientific value are the two Gvozdev reports: one given to Czarist Elizabeth in 1743 from Okhotsk and the other from Irkutsk in 1758. These documents, written for different reasons, tell about the most important events in Gvozdev's life. The information contained in these reports is confirmed by journals, reports of Russian sailors who sailed with Gvozdev, by reports of the Siberian Government and other materials.

*   *

*

In 1716, Mikhail Spiridonovich Gvozdev enrolled in Slavic-Greek-Latin Academy. Being founded in the second half of the seventeenth century, they taught mostly bible. Some mathematics and human sciences augmented the curriculum by the end of that century. The academy played a positive role in the distribution of knowledge in Russia.

The year 1701 saw the founding of the Mathematical-Navigational School in Moscow. Fourteen years later Peter the Great established the Naval Academy in St. Petersburg for the purpose of training professionals for the army and navy.

In 1718 Gvozdev began attending the Naval Academy where he remained a student until 1721."[15] A large number of students attended the geography course preparing cartographers.

Mathematics received the greatest emphasis in the Naval Academy as "the strongest foundation" of all the disciplines taught there. On January 11, 1719, Peter the Great issued a decree stating, "True solutions and proof depend upon mathematical skills. Being without them is like a tree without a root. People in government scientific positions who do not have a mathematics background will simply be forgotten."[16] During this time English professor Pharvarson served in Russia teaching at the Academy. He was a very talented man with a great deal of knowledge in many areas of science. He successfully taught arithmetic, geometry, trigonometry, astronomy, geography, navigation, cartography and the use of navigator's journals.

47

To the American Coast

Using Pharvarson's resources, Gvozdev learned the complicated geodesist profession.

Professor Pharvarson carefully monitored the achievements of Russian and foreign scientists. He taught his students the necessity of gaining scientific knowledge.

Another of Gvozdev's teachers was Russian scientist L. Magnitski, author of the book, *Arithmetic: The Numerical Science.*

In 1719, according to a decree of Peter the Great, the first graduating class went to various areas to work on the preparation of maps of Russia.

Successfully graduating from the Naval Academy in 1721, Gvozdev went to Novgorod for description of rivers and army infantry camps "and was so assigned until 1725."

Gvozdev returned to the Naval Academy in 1725 to continue his education. In 1727, as Gvozdev relates, he was examined by Professor Pharvarson and "became a geodesist."[17]

He soon had his chance to practice his theoretical and practical skills in a distant and not well known land. Having heard a lot about the Far East, Gvozdev was attracted by the mystery of the region. He also understood the possible difficulties, and, as did many of his colleagues, willingly used the opportunity and went east.

Soon after the expedition under Bering reached Kamchatka, an Yakutian Cossack leader by the name of Afanacy Shestakov arrived in St. Petersburg. He was a strong willed man, rich in practical experience, energetic, and at the same time egotistical, rude and power loving. While he couldn't read or write he did know a great deal about Siberia and the Far East, some of which he learned first hand and some he learned from others. Shestakov remembered everything that he saw. Then, based upon his memory, he would tell others of the "country and rivers he had seen or heard about and they, in turn, would draw maps based upon Shestakov's descriptions," writes historian Muller.

One of these maps was delivered to St. Petersburg under Shestakov's name. The map was not complicated and did not show Cape Chukota and the islands correctly. Muller writes, "the map of Shestakov was far from perfect."[18]

But in spite of its errors, the map provides valuable geographic and economic information. The map shows the Big Land, the eastern portion of Cape Dezhnev and groups of islands. Adjacent to Anadyr Gulf is a note, "on this island there are many people." (St. Lawrence Island). Also depicted are the Kuril Islands and a number of the islands of Japan. All of the locations of the map are primitive and inexact, of course. But at the same time it demonstrates that the Siberian Government possessed a lot of information about the farthest regions of northeast Asia. The main point is that the map provided economic information. There is a note on Karaginski Island, located adjacent to the mouth of the Kamchatka River: "The people on this island are called Kargi. They are independent and have many animals." Near one island in the Okhotsk Sea is a note: "Bear Island, there are many sables on this island."

German historian L. Breitfuss noticed the great historical value of Shestakov's map. Comparing it with previous maps he writes, "It was more exact but at the same time a strange representation of Northeastern Asia. It became known only in 1726 when the map, prepared by Cossack leader Afanacy Shestakov, appeared in St. Petersburg. On the map was shown Kamchatka, the northern portion the Big Land (America) and the Kuril Islands as described by Evreinov and Luzhin."

In this manner, the map indicates that the Siberian Government had a lot of information about that remote land. Obviously, the map attracted the attention of those in the Russian Government who were thinking about the colonization of Siberia and the Far East.

Understanding the necessity for serious research of the natural resources of that land, Shestakov asked to "examine the islands between Kamchatka and Japan,[19] and those adjacent to the mouth of the Amur River.[20] According to the information furnished by Japanese who came to Kamchatka in 1710, Shestakov was assured that there were "treasures buried on those islands."[21]

He sent a proposal with the map to the Senate to organize an expedition. Shestakov asked permission "to go with the expedition to Kamchatka to conquer the people living there, and to search for new islands and lands in order to join them to Russia." The proposal included the reconnaissance of the west coast of Okhotsk Sea and the coastal islands up to the Chinese border; discovery of a direct route from Udsk ostrog through the Okhotsk Sea to the west coast of Kamchatka; examination of the Kuril Islands; and the organization of a voyage from Southern Lopatka, Cape Kamchatka, to Anadyr. In addition, the project included consideration of a voyage to the coast of the Big Land located opposite the Chukchi Peninsula.

In the capital, Shestakov initiated energetic activity. His stories about the treasures of Kamchatka and the nearby islands gained the interest of influential people in the government. His project was warmly received by Kirilov, over-secretary of the Senate.

It was not long before the Senate suggested the Secret Supreme Soviet organize an expedition parallel to the one of Bering. In March, 1727, the Senate adopted a decree which said the lands situated close to Russia "would not be difficult to make part of our territory." The Senate decree also mentioned the good possibilities of fur trade. The conditions for sailing in the Kamchatka region were noted to be better than in the Arctic Ocean "because the Eastern Sea is warm not icy." Also expressed was the possibility of the establishment of commercial relations with Korea and Japan.

But the most important task of the expedition was the reconnaissance of the Shantar Islands. The decree said, "to send Russian explorers to the Shantar Islands to find out what people were living there and what kind of animals there were and whose possession were the islands, the Chinese or someone else."[22]

The new expedition to the Far East had broader tasks assigned to it than the Bering Expedition. According to Kirilov, by sending Bering to Kamchatka, Peter the Great thought "that it would bring just one form of news, whether or not Asia and America were connected. But about the present expedition, one did not know what news to expect." That was why the Czar "tried to find someone sufficiently interested to search for new lands and commercial opportunities."[23]

The government calculated the cost of the expedition that was to be headed by Afanacy Shestakov. They considered both Shestakov's and Bering's expeditions to be working on the same task of exploring the Northeastern region of the country. That is why the leaders of the two expeditions were to assist each other.

In 1727, Shestakov went from St. Petersburg to Okhotsk. Captain Pavlutski, with 400 Cossacks, joined him in Tobolsk. In Pavlutski's command was Mikhail Gvozdev who was assigned to the expedition by the Senate. J. Gens and I. Fedorov were sent by the Admiralty College, appropriately equipped. Also sent were 10 sailors and Ivan Speshnev from Kazan who was a ship specialist assigned to oversee ship construction in Okhotsk.

Gvozdev and mariner Ivan Fedorov went from Tobolsk to Okhotsk, arriving in 1729. During this time work in preparation of the expedition began in Okhotsk. Shestakov was a man of strong character who loved power. He did not want to share his power with Pavlutski. In his reports, Shestakov referred to Pavlutski in "not all too appropriate terms."[24] Pavlutski, for his part, was constantly writing reports about Shestakov.

On September 16, 1728, the Tobolsk Regional Chancellery wrote, "That you, Pavlutski and Shestakov, have not been assigned to the expedition to write reports about each other. These disagreements and disorder are delaying the expedition." At the same time he ordered the progress of the expedition to proceed more quickly "under threat of severe penalty."

All questions of Shestakov and Pavlutski were to be solved by mutual agreement. "If we punish anyone from the expedition, you Captain and Shestakov will be in the same situation. And you, Shestakov, cannot punish the servicemen without the Captain's agreement. According to the aforementioned decree, you are the first in command and he, Shestakov, the second." That notice is quite interesting. The Tobolsk Regional Chancellery was putting Pavlutski at the head of the expedition and assigning Shestakov as his assistant. But Shestakov didn't want to share power with anyone and referred to the decree of the Czar. The Tobolsk Regional Chancellery demanded a copy of the decree and ordered Pavlutski to act in strict compliance with it.[25]

In Pavlutski's order dated July 11, 1729, to mariners J. Gens and I. Fedorov and ship specialist I. Speshnev, he stressed the idea that he, Pavlutski, and Shestakov must conduct all affairs by mutual agreement.

In 1729, Shestakov dispatched Ivan Shestakov and 60 members of the expedition from Okhotsk on the *St. Gabriel* which had been left there by Bering. On the *Fortuna*, built by Galkin, Shestakov sent his son Vasilii with 20 Russian to Bolsheretsk ostrog. But Afanacy Shestakov himself left on the *Eastern Gabriel* for Tauisk ostrog.

Shestakov directed Gvozdev and Speshnev to go from Okhotsk to Tauisk and then to Koriak country and to wait for him there. But Gvozdev and Speshnev "did not make it because of snow storms and returned to Tauisk." Not waiting for Gvozdev and Speshnev, Shestakov continued his travel with a small group in 1730. Included among those in the expedition were 100 Tungus. They went through most of the Koriak country collecting tribute (yasak) from the inhabitants. It was learned that before the arrival of the expedition, the Chukchi had attacked the Koriaks. Upon reaching the Chukchi, a battle ensued "during which Shestakov and his men were defeated. Afterwards the Chukchi returned to their land." Following Shestakov's death during the battle, Pavlutski took over leadership of the expedition.

Pavlutski learned of Shestakov's death on April 25. The next day he directed J. Gens, I. Fedorov, I Speshnev and Gvozdev to take "the ship Bering left in Okhotsk and sail to Kamchatka. From Kamchatka they were to sail at once to Anadyr ostrog."

But if the ship is not there, take any ship available and "come to us here at Anadyr as quickly as possible." Gens was directed to take some sailors with him and have authority over them. It is important to mention that Pavlutski paid careful attention to the planning. He thought that it was necessary to expedite the campaign. That is why the message about the urgent preparations were sent to Okhotsk.

In Pavlutski's order sent to Gens and Fedorov in October, 1730, they were to take sailors, Ivan Shestakov and the personnel with him, seaman Prokophy Nagibin and Nikita Shevirin and the sailors who had participated in Bering's voyage. They were to "have accord with Shestakov in all matters without any arguments. They were to conduct their affairs by mutual agreement and not according to their own wills so that there would be agreement in the future." The assignments of the expedition, as Shestakov explained were not only for scientific tasks but economic and political as well. (They were to bring the native peoples under the authority of Russia, collect tribute from them and utilize them in hunting and furring.)

Speshnev and Gvozdev were assigned to the expedition as was Peter Shestakov if he arrived from Yakutsk by that time. According to the Czar's decree of April 30, 1730, and Pavlutski's order, Peter Shestakov was to go to the Yakutian Military Chancellery and receive provision and to bring them together with those at Anator Crossing to Okhotsk. Ivan Shestakov was directed to gather the sailors, soldiers and servicemen remaining from V. Shestakov's portion of the expedition and bring the artillery reserves from Okhotsk to Anadyr ostrog "at once."[26] In this way, Pavlutski's orders determined the exact organization and structure of the expedition.

On September 19, 1730, Gvozdev and Fedorov sailed from Okhotsk on the ship *St. Gabriel* under the command of navigator Gens. They arrived in Bolsheretsk on September 25 and remained there until the following summer. In July, 1731, the *St. Gabriel* sailed from Bolsheretsk to the mouth of the Kamchatka River. From there the sailors went to Nizhne-Kamchatka. Unfortunately, these voyages were not useful. Eight years later in Tobolsk, Gvozdev told the Siberian authorities that because of Gen's eye illness and Fedorov's leg problem, descriptions and maps were not completed.[27]

At Nizhne-Kamchatsk, preparations for the distant voyage were begun by repairing sails and preparing provisions and the necessary materials. Gens applied at the revenue collection building for provisions of 2,000 Yukola fish and 1,000 fresh red salmon, and interpreters Andrew Orlin, Evdokim Varipaev, Spirodon Perebyashin, Fyodor Zyryanov and Mikhail Shavoronov for the expedition.

In response to Gens' request, on July 13, shop assistant I. Kriskov informed him that "there were no reserves" in Nizhne-Kamchatsk ostrog. According to the servicemen there and the native people "on the Kamchatka River, at its mouth and on other rivers something had happened to the salmon and they could not supply the fish. The people were in great need and the only fish there was to eat was a small fish called Hahalchya."[28] I. Kriskov promised to supply the expedition with flour. He would also supply the interpreters if they could be located.

The *St. Gabriel* was scheduled to sail north on July 20, 1731, but did not make the voyage due to a rebellion by the Kamchadals. Gens was to sail north to Anadyr and then go to the islands. Soon Gens became ill, however, and mariner I. Fedorov became leader of the voyage.

The expedition was also charged to search for metals and jewelry stones; yashma, yahowt and hollandian. S. Gardelbol who, in Russian service at this time, was assigned to perform this work.

Pavlutski developed the program of scientific research for the expedition which was presented in his order of May 1, 1732. He included the issues from the First Bering Expedition. First of all they were supposed to find out who the people were who came to Bering's ship when he was near the Chukchi peninsula in 1728 and where they were from.

This program was very distinctive by its broad ideas and clear understanding of the purpose of the expedition. "We were ordered," wrote Mikhail Gvozdev in his report of September 1, 1743, to "go with the sailors and former sailors on the ship *Gabriel* around Cape Kamchatka to the mouth of the Anadyr River and to the land adjacent which is called the Big Land; and to find out what people lived there, "observe and search and take tribute from such people from whom tribute had never been received before, and to do the best we could."

*   *

*

The spring of 1732 arrived. The sailors were finishing the last preparations for the expedition, a long and difficult voyage. Everyone understood that it would be a big challenge because they were to travel to a previously unexplored region. The seafarers did not have any elementary maps of the area into which they were going. Included in the crew was an experienced sailor named Kondrati Moshkov, who had participated in Bering's Expedition. The sailors of the *Gabriel* put high hopes on Moshkov and called him their *kormchiy* (one who always seems to know the direction to go).

On July 23, 1732, the ship *Gabriel* sailed out of the mouth of the Kamchatka River. Four days later they passed Cape Kamchatka. On August 3, the ship reached the mouth of the Anadyr River from where the ship headed to "search for islands."[29] They decided to go to the island discovered by Bering in 1728. Seaman Moshkov showed the course of the ship And "through that seaman they went in search of the island and came to the south side of Cape Chukchi on August 5."[30]

It was not possible to continue the voyage for a while because of the lack of wind. Accordingly, they dropped anchor. They used the time of the unexpected to examine the coast. Gvozdev went ashore in a small boat for observations and fresh drinking water. The sailors went into a small river they discovered. They did not notice any signs of human habitation the first day. But soon the visitors noticed a deer herd with two herdsmen who ran away as soon as they saw the sailors.

To the American Coast

After filling two barrels with water, the sailors came back to the ship. On August 6, two kayaks came out from a bay, each with two men. Through interpreters, the natives were invited aboard the ship. "But they did not answer and, after looking over the ship, the natives returned to shore."

The next day, Gvozdev and a group of sailors headed into the bay from which the natives had come in their kayaks. They found two old yurts (semi-subterranean dwellings) made from whale bones. When nothing else of interest was discovered the sailors returned to the ship. During their three-day stay near the Chukchi Peninsula, the travelers managed to make some interesting observations.

Early on the morning of August 8 they resumed their voyage again as the wind was blowing in the right direction. The route of the ship was made in accordance with the suggestions of Moskov. The main purpose of the expedition was to reach the Big Land. However, on the next day, Fedorov became hesitant to continue the voyage and they returned to the place they had previously dropped anchor. Then by mutual agreement, the *St. Gabriel* turned back once more and on August 9, dropped anchor again, this time along the coast to the north. On August 13, they anchored near Cape Dezhnev because of a lack of wind. From there, they could see some structures. Gvozdev went ashore with a group of sailors where they found six yurts. At that moment they noticed a kayak headed towards the yurts. Considering this to be an attack, Gvozdev gave the order for the servicemen to return to the ship. Returning with 20 men, the Chukchi moved away from their shelters when they saw the Russians.

Gvozdev sent one serviceman with an interpreter for the purpose of asking the Chukchi to live under the jurisdiction of Russia. The Chukchi responded that "they did not know about tribute and would not pay." Again Gvozdev sent an interpreter to the Chukchi. Finally they asked the interpreter to bring a Russian to whom they would pay with parkas. Gvozdev then sent serviceman E. Permiakov to them with an interpreter. The Chukchi asked Permiakov to give them a knife and promised to give him a parka made of marten fur in exchange. Then the native chief said to the interpreter, "About this tribute you keep mentioning, I am the most powerful among all my people and have an important name. We had a battle with your captain." About this time the chief started jabbing the interpreter with a spear.

The battle to which the chief was referring took place July 14, 1731, between Pavlutski's men and the Chukchi. This increased the negative attitude of the native people toward the Russian government. This is the reason the natives and their chief met the sailors of the *St. Gabriel* with distrust and fear. It complicated the situation for the expedition. In spite of this the sailors made valuable observations of Chukchi life and activity and about the natural conditions on the Chukchi Peninsula during their stay on the coast. Gvozdev determined that the natives ate whale meat and walrus, "besides which I did not see any other provisions." Accordingly, the hunting of marine mammals was the main source of nutrition for the Chukchi.

Characterizing the natural conditions of the peninsula, the explorer noticed that there were no forests, "only tundra". For this time, Gvozdev's observations of the natives were very valuable from a scientific point of view.

Soon after the sailors came back to the ship the calm changed to a good wind. Not losing a valuable moment, the *St. Gabriel* continued its voyage August 15. Then on

August 16 and 17, they observed an island; it was probably Ratmanov island.

By this time the weather became calm again and the *St.
Gabriel* had to return to the Chukotka coast. They noticed
some yurts on the cape and sent some men ashore in a
small boat. The Chukchi left when they saw Gvozdev and
the other Russians. The first attempt to communicate
with the natives was unsuccessful. After a while they saw
kayaks on the horizon headed toward the *St. Gabriel.*
There were about 20 people in each boat. They refused to
come close to the ship but willingly started to talk with
the Russians. They said that they lived on Chukchi Peninsula and called themselves Big Tooth Chukchi.

All of this information, notes L.S. Berg, shows that the
St. Gabriel was near Cape Dezhnev in the vicinity of the
Eskimo village of Nuukna.

Finally, a wind came up and the ship sailed to Ratmanov Island where it had been only a few days earlier. Approaching from the north, sailors went ashore under the
leadership of Gvozdev. As the boat approached the island,
the Eskimos "suddenly started shooting and we responded
by firing three flintlock guns over their heads. We told the
interpreter to ask them what people they were," Gvozdev
writes. The Eskimos answered that they were Chukchi and
said "that their relatives had fought against the Captain's
forces and had beaten them all."

Gvozdev asked the islanders about the Big Land but
did not receive any significant information. However, the
Eskimos did say that "our Chukchi" lived on the Big
Land. They were called Big Chukchi. By this time the
islanders came out of their yurts, being assured that they
were not in danger. They willingly continued the conversation.

The Russian sailors went ashore where they found two wooden yurts built into the ground. Walrus and whale meat were present. After examining the lodgings the sailors returned to the ship. The *St. Gabriel* sailed to the south side of the island where there were about 20 yurts. Attempts to collect tribute from the natives were not successful.

The *St. Gabriel* dropped anchor on the south side of the island near the yurts. Again Gvozdev went ashore with some of the servicemen. Here there were many more yurts than on the north side of the island. The interpreter started a conversation with one of the Chukchi. When he asked about the Big Land and the people who lived there, the Chukchi did not answer directly. After this unsuccessful attempt to gain information about the Big Land, the sailors returned to the ship. Gvozdev reported that the island was small and that it was without trees.

On August 20, the voyage was continued but the lack of wind stopped them again. The ship was near a second island located about a half a mile from the first. It was determined that it was a smaller island and that it was inhabited. On August 21, the *St. Gabriel* sailed to the Big Land -- to Cape Prince of Wales. Approaching the coast, they dropped anchor. To their surprise they did not see anyone on the coast. So Fedorov ordered the ship to be headed south and soon the travelers noticed some yurts along the coast located about 1.5 versts apart.

The sailors finally arrived at the land they had heard so much about. On maps, it had been represented only by a big white spot. To solve the mystery of the big white spot was the only aspiration of the crew of the *St. Gabriel*. They tried to get closer to the land but a strong wind prevented them from doing so. The *St. Gabriel* sailed south along the land as Gvozdev carefully observed. The direction of the ship was headed toward the beach so they had to turn back. Soon the wind began blowing from the north and the navigator directed the ship be sailed to the southwest. The *St. Gabriel* approached an island on August 22 but "because of bad weather they could not drop anchor." The wind became so strong that they had to take down all the sails. It became stormy and they lost control of the ship as it was being carried away from the island. Some of the sailors said that because the season was late it was necessary to return to Kamchatka. Gvozdev responded by saying, "that is why we have a navigator. We cannot do anything without his agreement."[31]

By this time á Chukchi came to the ship in a small kayak -- kukhta. The kukhta was made of leather including the top. There was only space for one a man in it. The upper part of his dress was a shirt made of whale intestine. The shirt was connected to the kayak and covered his hands and feet. The sailors also noticed "a big bubble tied to the kayak so the waves could not turn it over."

The boat was similar to those indicated in Chirikov's reports. The Chukchi went to sea in such boats in fair weather. Answering the questions of the interpreter, the Chukchi willingly told that Chukchi lived on the Big Land and that there were pine forests there. They also learned about the animals that lived in the Big Land. Gvozdev noted that there were deer, marten, fox and river beaver. That information had scientific value. Now they had a more or less clear picture of the Big Land.

As soon as the Chukchi departed, servicemen Efim Permiakov, Laurenti Poliakov, Feyodor Paranchin, and Alexy Malyshev approached Gvozdev "asking to return to Kamchatka because of low provisions and water."

We cannot leave this question without addressing the issue that it raises. In all probability, they were under the leadership of Gvozdev which required them to assist him with the scientific research, but Fedorov was the commander of the ship. Fedorov and Gvozdev probably had equal rights. Gvozdev's response to the servicemen's inquiry demonstrates this: "I told them that we cannot go without the agreement of the navigator."

By this time the situation on the ship became complicated. The ship's provisions were nearly exhausted. Remaining in this area any longer could have resulted in disastrous consequences. The results of the expedition would be lost to science. "The sailors and servicemen gave the navigator and me a petition in which they addressed their needs and requested we return to Kamchatka because of these needs and the lateness of the season." In response to this petition, Gvozdev writes, the *St. Gabriel* returned to the mouth of the Kamchatka River on September 28."

During the voyage Gvozdev and Fedorov made notes in the ship's journal which Gvozdev sent to Okhotsk on July 22, 1733. The absence of complete agreement between the two leaders was evident in the information collected during the expedition. It also complicated the task of preparing a map of the voyage.

On June 22, 1733, Gvozdev wrote to the Okhotsk Chancellery with disappointment. His boss had made it impossible to prepare a map from the journal "because I was not allowed access to the journal for two days after we left Kamchatka."[32]

Further, Gvozdev writes, "even more, there were no any entries in the journal during many of the periods Fedorov was on duty." Gvozdev understood very well the value of accurate note taking. That is why he was displeased that he did not have an opportunity to use these skills and knowledge to research Northwest America. "And I would do the work according to my position and prepare the map as I was assigned."[33]

In spite of all the negative things that occurred during the voyage, it was a positive step forward compared to Bering's first expedition. The voyagers had been on islands in the Bering Strait which were later named for Gvozdev. Bering crossed the strait from north to south and Fedorov and Gvozdev crossed it from west to east. According to the voyager's information, the approximate time necessary to travel from Cape Chukchi to the Big Land was determined.

The final results of the voyage say that although Fedorov was ill, he did successfully lead the ship under complicated navigational conditions (islands, shallow water, foul weather). This was possible because of his good marine training and his skills as a sailor. Gvozdev, who had been in charge of the voyage, understood better than Fedorov its scientific purpose. He was a very active man. Several times during the voyage Mikhail Spiridonovich walked on Cape Chukchi and islands. The descriptions of the voyage which he made are the first witness of this remarkable feat. Based upon these documents scientists have restored, though not completely, the history of this heroic journey.

Based upon the reports of Gvozdev and Ilia Skurikhin, one of the participants in the expedition, the Okhotsk Chancellery reported to the Irkutsk Chancellery, " according to the above information you can get from the mouth of the Anadyr River to the Big Land in five days and from Cape Chukchi within one and a half days." At the end of the report, Okhotsk commander Devier expressed the

opinion that Bering should build small boats on the Anadyr River "as it is called a *shitik*, or something like that,
go there and search because of the great interest. And
without any doubt the Big Land is part of America."[34]

A. Chirikov, S. Malygin, D. Laptev, D.Ovtsyn, S. Hit-
rov and I. Elagin used the scientific results of the expedition in the preparation of a map of the northeastern part of
the Russian Empire. This map was finished in 1746. In
the description with the map is mentioned that "the land
located to the east of Cape Chukchi from 65° N. latitude
was transferred from the map of geodesist Gvozdev."[35]

During the first voyage to America, Russian sailors
collected interesting material about climatic and meteor-
itic conditions and about the fauna and flora of the north-
eastern portions of the Pacific Ocean. The research of the
native peoples of the Chukchi Peninsula and the Big Land
had significant value in spite of its nonsystematic form..

The experience gained by sailors during this expedition
was used by Chirikov and Bering during their voyages to
the Northeast American coast. Among the crews of the *St.
Peter* and *St. Paul* were many persons who participated in
the Gvozdev and Fedorov expedition. Mikhail Gvozdev
took part in the Second Siberian-Pacific Ocean Expedition, about which there is hardly any mention in the liter-
ature. But before that, Gvozdev had to overcome many
shortages and difficulties.

Fedorov died in 1733. Gvozdev was sent to Nizhne-
Kamchatsk to participate in reconstruction of the ostrog
until 1735. In that same year, navigator Gens and Gvozdev were arrested on false charges brought by Leonti
Petrov. They were sent to Tobolsk. Soon the nature of the
charges was understood and Petrov was punished. In 1738

the Admiralty College reviewed the cases against Gens and Gvozdev and decided they were not guilty.

Accordingly, they "ordered a decree be issued concerning the above mentioned Gens and Gvozdev case, to set them free, to pay their back wages, to send Gens to the Kamchatka Expedition of Captain-Commander Bering, and Gvozdev to his previous Assignment."[36] "And in the same year," writes Gvozdev, "I was released according to the decree received from the Admiralty College and sent to the Irkutsk Chancellery; and in May 1739, I was sent to Okhotsk to join Gregory Skorniakov's crew."[37] In Okhotsk Gvozdev worked as a geodesist until 1741.

In the same year, according to Captain William Walton,[38] Gvozdev was directed to describe the coast of the Okhotsk Sea from the mouth of the Okhota River to the south, "to Udskaya side, which I described according to the instructions given to me by the captain."

Soon Gvozdev was assigned to Spanberg's crew which was going on a voyage to Japan.

Spanberg was directed to establish friendly relations with Japan and to investigate the possibility of becoming trading partners. It was recommended to Spanberg and his officers to "talk nicely and tell them that besides the land of the Russian Empire, Siberia extends to the sea in the vicinity of Japan and to have friendly relations with each other could result in significant profit."[39] The fleet was assigned a variety of scientific tasks: description of the sea routes, meteorological and navigational studies, and becoming familiar with the life styles, customs and traditions of the Japanese people.

The preparations for the expedition were very slow and were not completed until September. In all, four ships were prepared including the double-sloop *Nadezhda*. The time that it would have been convenient for a voyage from Okhotsk Sea was lost resulting in the cancellation of the expedition for that year. Spanberg sent three of the ships to Kamchatka and the *Nadezhda*, under the leadership of Shelting and Gvozdev, to describe the west coast of the Okhotsk Sea to the mouth of the Amur River.

On September 4, the double-sloop went to sea. Proceeding along the coast, the *Nadezhda* approached the Shantar Islands within 5 days. Gvozdev took careful notes and recorded them in the journal.

On September 7, the sailors sighted Takol Island near the mouth of the Aldan River. On September 10, the weather was changing to calm and clear. The sailors carefully observed unknown places, measuring the water's depth, determining the nature of the land and the direction and speed of the currents.

On September 11, about 7 o'clock, the *Nadezhda* lifted anchor and headed toward the mouth of the Uda River. In a half an hour, the depth of the sea was only five feet and it was dangerous to proceed any further. Mariner Rtishev, who was sent to measure the depth reported that "it was only three feet." In spite of the risks of sailing in such shallow depths, it was decided to continue. According to the advice of navigator Chepalov, they decided to keep to the right side of the river. Orientation was difficult because of poor visibility and soon the ship ran aground. "And navigator Chepalov directed the ship along the right side of the river where there was not a channel and we stopped on a sandbar. When the tide went out, we saw a channel on the left side of the river."[40] Shelters built by the native population were observed along the shore.

On September 13, the *Nadezhda* left the mouth of the Uda River which they determined to be at 55⁰ 30' No.

latitude. In that they had observed that the depth of the river did not exceed three feet, their research showed that it was too shallow for use by ocean going vessels. They also noted there were not any usable forests in the area nor was the land suitable for agricultural purposes. On September 15, Gvozdev took two boats to Udsk ostrog while the remainder of the crew made observations concerning the river and its many tributaries. There are many similar detailed notes in the expedition's documents.[41] On September 21, Shelting and Gvozdev returned from Udsk ostrog.

From September 22 to the 28th, the double-sloop *Nadezhda* sailed among the Shantar Islands seeking a suitable anchorage. They were unsuccessful. By this time the ship started leaking and was threatened. It was very risky to continue the voyage. Accordingly, they decided to sail to Bolsheretsk where they arrived on October 9. In this manner, in the campaign of 1741 the crew of the *Nadezhda* described the mouth of the Uda River and Shantar Islands. But the fleet did not accomplish its assigned task of sailing to Japan.

Bering and Chirikov received the scientific results of the remarkable voyage to the American coast. On July 16, 1741, the packet-boat *St. Paul* under the leadership of A. E. Chirikof reached Alaska near an island called Baker ($55^0 21$'N.L.). During this voyage near the American coast (until July 27) they observed and put 400 versts of the coast of Alaska on the map. On their return to Kamchatka Chirikov discovered the Aleutian Islands.

A day and a half after Chirikov, Bering also reached the American coast on the packet-boat *St. Peter* at the latitude of $58^0 14$'N. On their return they discovered the Ukamok Islands, a small group of islands call Evdokeevski, part of the Shumigan and Aleutian Islands. However, these remarkable voyages were at great cost.[42]

During the winter of 1741-2, the Spanberg portion of the expedition was preparing their ships for the voyage of May 2, 1742. Gvozdev was appointed to the double-sloop *Nadezhda*. "We are sending to you M.S. Gvozdev," Spanberg wrote to Rtishev, "to assist you and to make notes in your journal. Gvozdev is a geodesist."[43]

The commander of the *Nadezhda* was mariner Kozin and the navigator was Basil Rtishev. They had a crew of 33 persons and provisions for five months. On May 23, the fleet left the mouth of the Bolsheretsk River under the leadership of Spanberg and headed towards the Kuril Islands.

The main purpose of the voyage was to reach Japan. Spanberg directed the commanders of the ships to show signs of good will if they met the Japanese at sea. Spanberg's instructions of May 14, 1742 to Shelting on the *Arkhangel Mikhail* read in part, "establishing friendship on land will be impossible if we show hostility at sea."[44]

On the third day of the voyage, they reached the first of the Kuril Islands. They took some of the native peoples from these islands to act as interpreters. On May 30, they resumed the voyage and headed in a southeasterly direction. The weather was cloudy. During the next few days it became foggy. The ships lost sight of each other because the equipment those days was primitive and the sailors were inexperienced. Strong frontal winds complicated the situation. Of all the ships, the *Nadezhda* achieved the best results.

After becoming separated, the *Nadezhda* reached a latitude of $46^0 21'$N. before returning to the Kuril Islands, where it arrived July 21 a few days ahead of the packet-boat *St. Joann.*

Spanberg appointed mariner Shelting[45] as commander of the double-sloop and directed him to go to the Okhotsk Sea and continue with the description of the west coast from the Uda River to the mouth of the Amur River. The remainder of the ships returned to the Kuril Islands and proceeded to Bolsheretsk for maintenance.

On July 24, the *Nadezhda* left the Kuril Islands and reached Sakhalin Island August 1 at a latitude of $50^0 10$'N. They initially thought it was Yesso Land. Heading south the sailors reached latitude $45^0 34$'N. and went into the strait that separates Sakhalin Island from Japan. At the end of the eighteenth century this strait was named after French explorer Laperouse. Strong winds and heavy fog complicated the voyage and the sailors were unable to see the coast even though they were only six miles from it.

During the voyage near the coast of Sakhalin the Russian sailors had been near the mouth of the Amur River. The *Nadezhda* skipper reported to Spanberg, "but because of strong winds, bad weather and fog, it was not possible to see it."[46]

Geodesist Gvozdev was responsible for several things. He continuously and carefully posted notes in the ship's journal, stood watch and made descriptions of the coast.

On August 20, the double-sloop turned back because the ship was leaking and provisions were in short supply. They described the eastern coast of Sakhalin on their return to Okhotsk where they arrived September 10, 1742. For three and a half months the *Nadezhda* was on a non-stop voyage during which time the double-sloop, built by ship specialist Kuzmin, showed itself as an enduring ship with good navigational qualities.

To the American Coast

In 1744, Spanberg wrote that during a number of years the ship made voyages and is "still strong and remains as does the *Mikhail*, and the *Nadezhda* was a comfortable and seaworthy vessel."

Many ships built by talented Russian specialists in the Far East made successful voyages to Japan, Northwest America and other remote places in the northeast part of the Pacific Ocean.

During the following years Gvozdev participated actively in solving scientific and economic problems. The significant geographic discoveries made by Russian sailors required additional study in order to be useful for economic development purposes. That is the reason various direct trade opportunities between Russia and Western European countries, the colonies in America, China, Japan and other Pacific Rim countries were established. But in order to accomplish this, it was necessary for Russia to have its own ship construction facilities in the Far East. As everyone knew, the Okhotsk port could not satisfy increased demand. Even during the Second Siberian-Pacific Ocean Expedition, many people suggested relocating the port at Okhotsk to another location.

In the spring of 1743, the Okhotsk Chancellery directed mariner Shelting to research the possibility of establishing a ship construction facility on the Marikan River. Shelting directed Rtishev and Gvozdev to accomplish this task. In their report to Shelting of July 7, 1743, they wrote it was possible to build a base on the Marikan River but it would be impossible for ships to go from there to the Okhotsk Sea because of the shallowness of the water. Even during periods of high water, the current was very fast and had many shallow places. The depth of the river was 9, 6 and 3 feet and less.

The report of Gvozdev and Rtishev indicates how carefully and thoughtfully its authors performed their duties. That document contains significant economic and geographic information.

To the American Coast

At the same time, local governments expressed an
interest in that portion of northwest America located adjacent to Cape Chukchi that was not examined by either
Bering or Chirikov. A new expedition was planned and it
was necessary to carefully study all the materials of Russia's first voyage to the Big Land. The instructions the
Okhotsk Chancellery issued in Spanberg's name on April
20, 1743, mentioned that information from Gvozdev
would allow them to have a clear representation of the
land he described during his voyage of 1732. Then, "the
accuracy of the geodesist's report about the islands and
the Big Land" could be established and small ships could
be sent to the American coast with a commander who
"really understood the science, marine practices and locations on maps."[48] The Okhotsk Chancellery paid particu-
lar attention to the selection of the head of the expedition,
one who had to have good theory and practical experience
in the maritime field and could place things examined on
maps with precision.

The preparation for the expedition was in its active
stage. The materials of Fedorov and Gvozdev were carefully examined.

On September 9, 1743, Captain Spanberg, in response
to an order from the Okhotsk and Irkursk Chancelleries,
directed mariners Yushin, Roditchev and geodesist Gvozdev to collect the information about the voyage of the *St.
Gabriel* from Kamchatka to Cape Chukchi and then to the
Big Land. It was ordered for them to prepare an extract
from the journals "about all that was described during the
voyage, the places visited, and to prepare a map."

This task had very serious implications and was complicated by the short period of time in which it was to

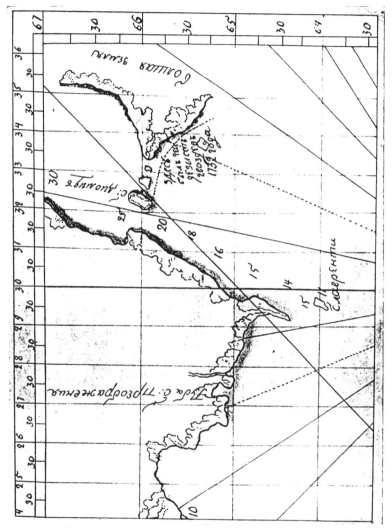

Portion of Gvozdev's Map from Efimov's Atlas of 1964

75

be accomplished. Considering the map to not be sufficiently accurate, Yushin wrote in his report to Spanberg on October 8, 1743, "It is difficult to attest to the accuracy of the prepared map from the Kamchatka River to Cape Chukchi and further islands, according to the journal kept by Fedorov because he did not post the notes all of the time." In spite of its lack of exactness, the map had significant scientific value. It summarized facts and materials gathered during the first voyage of Russian sailors to the American coast and it reflected the part of the Big land examined by Fedorov and Gvozdev.

In this way, the map prepared by Yushin, Roditchev and Gvozdev, "was presented to me after its completion with a report," writes Spanberg. According to these documents, we can say with certainty that the authors of the map published by correspondent-member A.V. Efimov in his work *The History of Russian Expeditions to the Pacific Ocean* under Spanberg's name are Yushin, Roditchev and Gvozdev.

The Irkutsk Provincial Chancellery planned to send an expedition to the Big Land. The expedition had various scientific, economic, political and social tasks. It had to determine the exact distance from Kamchatka to Chukotka to the Big Land and the islands near the Big Land. It was also to find out if there were any forests or usable bays, the size of the population, their religion and customs and "under whose jurisdiction they were or if they were independent and to whom did they pay tribute and how."[49] The expedition was to find out if there was any land or islands near the Big Land with people about whom "we don't know, and under whose protection they live, and the latitude of these places, and is there gold, silver or any other ore..."

The Okhotsk Chancellery recommended Gvozdev be sent on the expedition "because he was on these islands, and if we are going to send anyone, we should send Gvozdev."

Spanberg thought Gvozdev should not have been sent because he was working with materials of Chirikov's voyage, Bering's voyage and others. He would not be able to finish that work were he to go. In November, 1743, Spanberg was writing to the Irkutsk Chancellery, "it is not possible to send Mikhail Gvozdev to Okhotsk and separate him for membership in the expedition..."[50]

Although the expedition did not occur, the attempt to organize it is very interesting in that it reflects the various interests of local governments. Later, because of their initiative and support, many ships of traders would be sent making great contributions to the science of geography.

Spanberg's report of November, 1743 to the Okhotsk Chancellery is very interesting because it describes the various activities necessary to make an expedition successful. Spanberg wrote that if it was finally decided to send an expedition, it would be necessary to prepare a small ship with all the necessary equipment. The experience of previous voyages indicated that the commander of the ship had a most important role. He had to have good theoretical and practical knowledge of marine affairs "to determine the location of various places on maps." But even the best commander will not be able to solve the complicated task of controlling the ship without a good assistant. That is why Spanberg wanted asigned to him "a reliable person, because one will not be able to do everyhing by himself at sea." But even that was not enough. To make the voyage successful, they had to have well trained sailors. That is why Spanberg paid so much attention to sailors and soldiers "who will perform the same duties as the sailors." Also, Spanberg expressed valuable information related to the fact that the ship has to have enough provisions. "It is better to think to add something to the reserves than to have shortages at sea, because there (God save us), in places without food, everyone cannot survive." All these conclusions were accepted in subsequent Russian voyages.

Mikhail Gvozdev participated in the Second Siberian-Pacific Ocean Expedition for several years. He successfully used his knowledge of geography and marine science. He completed his assignments with great zeal. He described the coast of the Okhotsk Sea, prepared various maps, with great talent, made copies of maps, and during voyages to the mouth of the Amur River and Japan, "being on those voyages, performed not only his own duties," Gvozdev writes, "but also those of a navigator with great interest and desire."

*   *

*

The goverment did not appreciate Gvozdev's achievements. He was not promoted in rank or given a salary increase. This had a very negative effect on his morale. In
his report of August 24, 1743, to the Admiralty College,
Gvozdev wrote that after being in remote and dangerous
locations, "I still have the same rank while the other geodesists have been promoted."

After the expedition, Gvozdev went to Tomsk along
with the other members of the expedition in 1744 where
he lived for eleven years.

In 1755 Gvozdev then went to Irkutsk. There was a
plan to develop the economy of Eastern Siberia at that
time. The broad development of the maritime industry and
continuous voyages of Russian sailors to the Pacific and
Arctic Oceans demanded the development of agriculture
and animal husbandry. In addition, they also needed to
grow large amounts of hemp and flax for making sails.
Accordingly, many geodesists worked as surveyors. Mikhail Gvozdev recieved assignment for this work. He
worked in Irkutsk for three years. It was there he met F.I.
Soimonov, the famous scientist and explorer. He was one
of the first Russian hydrographers. Soimonov was
assigned as the General-Governor of Siberia in 1757.

F.I. Soimonov was very interested in the voyage of
Fedorov and Gvozdev. He wrote interesting details about
the voyage in his report to Catherine II dated November
23, 1757. He wrote, "in the above mentioned expedition
in 1732, during Skorniakov-Pisarev's time. Gvozdev was
sent on the expedition, which was near that land, though

he doesn't recall many of the details now and the journal of the voyage cannot be found, but he explained to me that he saw a lot of forests there."

In spite of his condition, he continued his work as a geodesist. He made descriptions of the villages on the Moscow road. He could not continue his work indefnite-ly. In 1758 he wrote, "because of my health and age and long period of service, I am asking for retirement." Siber-ian General-Governor F.I. Soimonov supported Gvoz-dev's request and assigned him employment tasks in Siberia according to his health condition. "Respectfully requesting," Soimonov wrote to the Senate for Gvozdev's retirement, "because of his illness and age and long ser-vice. And instead of Gvozdev, send another geodesist to finish Irkutsk Province and Nershinsk District and then work in the Siberia District when he is finished."[51]

No one knows anything about the further fate of first discoverer Gvozdev, but what we do know already gives us the right to say that he was an educated and hardwork-ing scientist who was strong willed and modest. He ignor-ed the hazards of many long voyages and served as an example for others. He was a willing worker.

Gvozdev was one of the most active participants in the great Russian discoveries in the Pacific Ocean that brought glory to Russia. That is why Gvozdev's name, as the name of many other famous Russian sailors, will always be fresh in the memory of our people.

III Footnotes

Introduction

[a] Muller, G.F. *Bering's Voyages: The Reports from Russia.* trans, C.L. Urness, University of Alaska Press: Fairbanks, 1986, pp. 1-2.

[11] Goldenberg, L.A. *Gvozdev: The Russian Discovery of Alaska in 1732.* ed. J.L.Smith, trans.N.M. Phillips and A.M. Perminov, Anchorage: Whitestone Press, 1990, p. 3.

[12] Hunt, W. *Arctic Passage.* New York: Charles Scribner's Sons, 1975, p.11.

[13] Golder, F.A. *Berings Voyages.* New York: Octagon Books, Inc., 1968, (originally published in 1922 by the American Geographical Society of New York) p.18.

[14] Urness, C.L. "Bering's First Expedition: A Re-examination Based on Eighteenth-century Books, Maps, and Manuscripts." Ph.D dissertation, University of Minnesota, 1982, p.113

[15] Berhk, V.N. *A Chronological History of the Discovery of the Aleutian Islands.* ed. R.A. Pearce, trans. D. Krenov, Kingston, Ontario: The Limestone Press, 1974, p. 24.

[16] Frost, O.W. ed., *Bering and Chirikov: The American Voyages and Their Impact.* Anchorage: Alaska Historical Society, 1992, p. 3.

[17] Dmytryshyn, B. Crownhart-Vaughan, E.A.P., Vaughan, T. ed. and trans., *Russian Penetration of the North Pacific Ocean 1700-1797.* Portland: Oregon Historical Society Press, 1988, pp. 132-3.

[18] Ibid., p.166

[19] Baker J.N.L. *A History of Geographical Discovery and Exploration*. Boston: Houghton Mifflin Co., 1931, p. 157., and Brebner, J.B. *The Explorers of North America 1492-1806*. London: A&C Black Ltd., 1933, p. 399

[110] Fisher, R.H. *Bering's Voyages: Whither and Why*. Seattle and London: University of Washington Press, 1977, p. 168

[111] Ibid., Dmytryshyn etc., p. 132.

[112] Polevoy, B.P. "The 250th Anniversary of the Discovery of Alaska." in *Polar Geography and Geology*, Vol. 7, July-Sept. 1983, p. 211

[113] Makarova, R.V. *Russians in the Pacific, 1743-1799*. Ed. and trans. by R.A. Pierce and A.S. Donnelly, Kingston: The Limestone Press, 1975, p. 17.

[114] Golder, F.A. *Russian Expansion on the Pacific 1641-1850*. Cleveland: The Arthur H. Clark Co., 1914, Appendix E

[115] Dobbs, A. ed. *A Letter from a Russian Sea-Officer, to a Person of Distinction at the Court of St. Petersburgh*. London: A. Linde, etc., 1754, p.67-8.

[116] Ibid., p. 22.

[117] Ibid., Muller, pp. 76-77.

[118] Ray, D.J. *The Eskimos of Bering Strait, 1650-1898*. Seattle and London: University of Washington Press, 1992, p. 25.

[119] Robertson, W. *The History of America*. London: W. Strahan; T. Cadell, 1777, Bk. IV, pp. 277-8.

[120] Coxe, W. *A Comparative View of the Russian Discoveries with those made by Captains Cook and Clerke*. London: J. Nichols, 1787, p.15.

[121] Burney, J. *Chronological History of North-Eastern Voyages of Discovery and of the Early Eastern*

Navigations of the Russians. London: Payne and
Foss, 1819, pp. 130-132

[122] Dall, W.H. *Alaska and Its Resources*. Boston: Lee and
Shepard, 1870, pp. 298-299.

[123] Bancroft, H.H. *History of Alaska*. New York: The
Bancroft Company, 1886 p. 39.

[124] Ibid., p. 40-41.

[125] Ibid., p. 79.

[126] Baker, M. *Geographic Dictionary of Alaska*. Washington: Government Printing Office, 1906, p. 218.

[127] Clarke, 1910, p. 1485

[128] Heawood, E. *A History of Geographical Discovery in
the Seventeenth and Eighteenth Centuries*. New
York: Octagon Books 1969 (reprint of 1912 ed.
published by Cambridge University Press), p. 260.

[129] Ibid., p. 261.

[130] Ibid., Golder, 1968, p.22.

[131] Ibid., Baker, J.N.L., p. 157.

[132] Ibid., Brebner, p. 399.

[133] Hulley, C.C. *Alaska: Past and Present*. Portland:
Binfords & Mort, 1970, p. 55.

[134] Ibid., Dobbs, p. 22.

[135] Ibid., Muller, p. 76.

[136] Ibid., Ray.

[137] Bagrow, L. "Ivan Kirilov, Compiler of the First
Russian Atlas, 1689-1737." *Imaga Mundi*, II 1938,
p. 81.

[138] Ibid., Polenoy, p. 212.

[139] Goldenberg, L.A. *Katorzhanin--sibirskii gubernator:
zhizn' i trudy F.I. Soimonova*. Magadan: Magadan
Publishing House, 1979, pp. 88-89.

[140] Ibid., Golder, 1914, Appendix E.

[141] Ibid.

[142] Ibid., Goldenberg, 1990, p. 36.

[143] Ibid., p. 37.

[144] Ibid., Goldenberg, 1990, pp.87-88.

[145] Ibid., p. 86.

[146] Ibid.

[147] Breitfuss, L. "Early Maps of North-Eastern Asia and of the Lands around the North Pacific: Controversy between G.F. Muller and N. Delisle." *Imago Mundi,* III, 1939, p. 94.

[148] Fisher, R.H. "The Early Carography of the Bering Strait Region," *Arctic*, Vol. 37, No. 4, Dec., 1984. p. 585.

[149] Ibid., Breitfuss, p. 94.

[150] Lanzeff, G.V., and Richard A. Pierce. *Eastward to Empire: Exploration and conquest on the Russian Open Frontier, to 1750.* Montreal: McGill-Queen's University Press, 1973, p. 94.

[151] Goldenberg, L.A. "'Geodesist Gvozdev was Here in 1732' (Eighteenth Century Cartographic Traditions in the Representation of the Discovery of Bering Strait." in *Polar Geography and Geology*, Vol. 7, July-Sept 1983, p. 215.

[152] Ibid., Breitfuss, p. 95

[153] Ibid., Muller, p. 52.

[154] Ibid., Goldenberg, 1990, p. 96.

[155] Ibid., Muller, 1986, p. 67.

[156] Ibid., p. 52.

[157] Ibid., Dmytryshyn, p.134.

[158] Alekseev, I. *The Destiny of Russian America 1741-1867.* ed. R.A. Pierce & trans. M. Ramsey, Kingston and Fairbanks: The Limestone Press, 1990, p.13.

[159] Ibid., Breitfuss, p. 99.

160   Ibid., Goldenberg, p. 219.

161   Ibid.

162   Khisamutdimov, A.A. "The Route of the St. Peter to America," in *Bering and Chirikov: The American Voyages and Their Impact*. ed. O.W. Frost, Anchorage: Alaska Historical Society, 1992, p.163

163   Ibid., Ray.

164   Ibid., Goldenberg, 1990, p. 40.

165   Ibid., Muller, pp.76-77.

166   Krashninnikov, S.P. *Explorations of Kamchatka, 1735-1741*. Trans. E.A.P. Crownhart-Vaughan, Portland: Oregon Historical Society, 1972, p. 315.

167   Ibid., Muller, p. 75.

168   Ibid., Lantzeff and Pierce, p. 212.

169   Ibid., Muller, p.75.

170   Ibid., Lantzeff and Pierce, p. 212.

171   Black, J.L. *G.-F. Muller and the Imperial Russian Academy*. Kingston and Montreal: McGill-Queen's University Press, 1986. pp. 134-135.

172   Ibid., Muller, p. 76.

173   Ibid., Golder, 1914, p. 156.

174   Ibid., Goldenberg, 1990, p. 39.

175   Ibid., Lantzeff and Pierce, pp. 211-212.

176   Ibid., Golder, 1914, p. 175. and Lantzeff and Pierce, p. 211.

177   Ibid., Golder, 1914, p. 156.

178   Ibid., Goldenberg, 1990,.p.40.

179   Ibid., Golder, 1914, p.156, Bancroft, p. 38 and Goldenberg, 1990, p. 76.

180   Ibid., Goldenberg, 1990, pp.40-41.

181   Ibid., Muller, p. 77.

182   Ibid., Golder, 1914, p.158.

183   Ibid., Goldenberg, 1990, p. 44.

[184] Divin, V.A. *K beregam Ameriki. Plavaniya i issledovaniya M. S. Gvozdeva, pervootkryvatelya Severo-Zapadnoy Ameriki*, Moscow: Geografgiz, 1956. p. 19.

[185] Ibid., Goldenberg, 1990, p. 41

[186] Ibid., p. 42.

[187] Ibid., Latzeff and Pierce, p. 212.

[188] Ibid., Goldenberg, 1990, p. 43.

[189] Ibid., Muller, p. 77.

[190] Ibid., Goldenberg, 1990, p. 44.

[191] Ibid., p. 47.

[192] Ibid., p. 48.

[193] Ibid., p. 49.

[194] Ibid., Krasheninnikov, p. 316-321.

[195] Ibid., Muller, p. 76.

[196] Ibid., Goldenberg, 1990, p. 54.

[197] Ibid., Andreev, p. 9.

[198] Ibid., pp. 9-10.

[199] Ibid., Goldenberg, 1990, p. 64.

[1100] Ibid., p. 67.

[1101] Ibid., Ray, p. 21 of the 1975 edition.

[1102] Svet, Y.M. and S.G. Fedorova, "Captain Cook and the Russians" *Pacific Studies*. VI, No. 1, Fall 1978, p. 9.

[1103] Ibid., Polevoy., p. 205.

[1104] Ibid., Goldenberg, 1983 p. 215.

[1105] Ibid., Akekseev, p. 12.

[1106] Shopotov, K.A., "The Year 1992 is the 260th Anniversary of the Russian Discovery of Alaska." in *Bering and Chirikov: The American Voyages and Their Impact.* ed. O.W. Frost. Anchorage: Alaska Historical Society, 1992, p. 156.

[1107] Holland, p. 98.

[1108] Falk, M.W. *Alaska.* World bibliograpical series; V. 183. Oxford, England; Santa Barbara Calif.: CLIO Press, 1995, p. 21.

[1109] Ibid., Ray, p. 21.

Translation

[1] Lomonosov, M.V. *Polnye sobrannyue sochineniya.* Vol. 1, p. 189.

[2] Forster, William Z., *Ocherki Politicheskoi istorii Ameriki*, St. Petersburg, 1953, p. 800.

[3] Golder, F.A., *Bering's Voyages*, New York, 1922, pp. 21-24.

[4] Breitfuss, L., "Early Maps of Northeaster Asia and of Lands Around the North Pacific," *Imago Mundi*, Vol. III, London, 1939, p.89.

[5] Polonski, A., "Pokhod geodezista Mikhaila Gvozdeva v beringov proliv," *Morskoi sbornik*, No. 11, St. Petersburg, 1850, p. 390.

[6] Ogloblin, N., "Die '*Shaski*' V.L. Atlasav ob otkry Kamchatka," *chteniya v obshestve istorii drevnostei rossiisknkh*, Moscovscom un-te, St. Petersburg, 1891, bk 3, p. 12.

[7] Gerye, V.I., "Otnoshenie Leybnits k Rossii I Petr elnkomu," po neizdannym bumagam v annoverskoi biblioteke cpb., St. Petersburg, 871 pp. 14 and 18; sm. "Takthe Sbornik pisem i memorialov Leybnits ot-nosyashikhsya v Rossii I Peter Velikomu," St. Petersburg, 1893, pp. 19-25.

[8] Gerye, V.I., "Otnoshenie Leybnits k Rossii," p. 126; "Sbornik pisem I memorialovLeybnits," p. 192.

[9] Gerye, V.I., "Otnoshenie Leybnits I Rossii i Peter Velikomu," pp. 146-147; sm. "Sbornik

pisem i memorialov Leybnits," pp. 248-249.

[10] Gerye, V.I., "Sbornik pisem i memorialov Leybnits", "Otnosyashikhsya Leybnits k Rossii i Velikomu," p. 360.

[11] I.K. Kirilov's Project, see Efimov, A.V., "Iz istorii velikikh geograficheskikh otkrytiy," *Geogrifgiz*, 1950, p. 289.

[12] Polonski, A., "Pokhod geodezista Mikhaila Gvozdev v beringa proliv," *Morskoi sbornik,* No. 11, 1850; Sokolov, A., "Pervyi pokhod russkikh k Amerike, 1732" *Zapiski gidrograficheskogo departamenta,* 1851, ch. IX.

[13] Berg, L.S., *Otkrytie Kamchatki i eksieditsii Beringa.* Bodnarskiy, M.S., *Ocherki po istorii risskogo zemlevedenia,* AN, SSSR, 1947, ch. 1, Izd. Perevalov, V.A., *Lomonosov i arktika,* Moscow, Leningrad: Glavsevmorput, 1949. Efimov, V.A., "Iz istorii russkikh ekspeditsii na tikhom okeane," *Geografgiz,* 1950. A. Zibin and Gvozdev's report to Captain Spanberg dated September 2, 1743, for analysis of these documents see: Efimov above pp. 236-249 and 153-155. Zubov, N.N., "Otechestveniye moreplavanie - issledovateli morey i okeanov," *Geografgiz,* 1954.

[14] "Documents concerning the voyage of Captain-Commander Bering to the American Coast in 1741" Chicago, 1893, pp. 3-4. (In Russian) characteristics of the documents presented by the Russian Government to the Colombian expedition; and original (English) correspondence of officials of the USA about the receiving of the original Bering report by the Russian Government.

[15] Central States Historical Archives, Leningrad,
Collection 1341, Section 303, Cases 485-6, 1764,
Part I, pages 399 and the other side.

[16] *Materialy po istorii russkogo flota,* Part 9, p. 536.

[17] Central States Archives of the Navy. Collection 216,
Part 1, Case 56, pages 983 and the other side, and
ibid., Central States Historical Archives.

[18] Muller, G.F., *Sochineniya I porevody, k polize
i uveseleniu sluthashie,* St. Petersburg, 1758,
ch.1 p. 200.

[19] He means Kuril Islands.

[20] He probably means Shantar Is. and Sakhalin Is.

[21] Original report of S. Gardelbol of July 4, 1731,
TsGADA. Senate Collection, Book 664, p. 88.

[22] *Polnoe sobranie zakonov Russiikoi imperii.* St.
Petersburg, Vol. VII, Page 772.

[23] Kirilov' Project, see Efimov, A.V., "Iz istorii russkikh
ekspeditsii na tikhom okeane," *Geografgiz,*
Moscow, 1950, p. 289.

[24] "Ekspeditsiia Beringa," Sbornik dokumentov,
Podgotovil k pechati, A. Pokrovski, St. Petersburg,
1941, p. 71.

[25] Ibid, pp. 72-3.

[26] Ibid., p. 75.

[27] M.S. Gvozdev Report of July 13, 1738, TsGAVMF,
Bering Collection, Book 24. p. 599 and the other
side.

[28] Hahalchya - a specie of rogatka fish. (S.P. Krasheninnikov, *Description of Kamchatka,* Vol.1, p. 308).

[29] Gvozdev's of September 2, 1743, see A.V. Efimov, *Iz
istorii russkikh ekspeditsii no tikhom okeane,*
Moscow, 1948, p. 245.

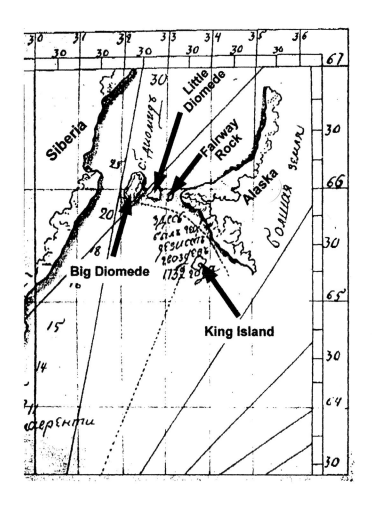

**Key to photos on following pages using
Gvozdev's map**

91

To the American Coast

The photograph on page 93 is of Little Diomede
(Kruzenshtren) Island in the foreground, Big
Diomede (Ratmanov) Island in behind it and the
Siberian coast in the background.
(Courtesy of Aeromap U.S.)

The photograph on page 95 is of Fairway Rock (Ukiyok
Island) with the Alaskan coast in the background.
(Courtesy of Aeromap U.S.)

The photograph on page 97 is of King Island and Village.
(Courtesy of the Anchorage Museum of History and Art)

[30] Berg, L.S., *Otkrytie Kamchatki eksieditsii Beringa, 1725-1742,* Moscow-Leningrad, 1946, p. 99.

[31] Gvozdev's of September 2, 1743, see A.V. Efimov, *Iz istorii russkikh ekspeditsii no tikhom okeane,* Moscow, 1948, p, 248.

[32] Central States Archives of the Navy, Bering Collection, Case 53, pp. 738 and the other side.

[33] Ibid.

[34] *Russkie otkrytiya v Tikhom okeane Severioy Amerike v XVIII veke.* i co vstupitelinoy statiey doktora istorichckikh nauka, A.N. Andreev, St. Petersburg: Geografgiz, 1948, p. 106.

[35] TsGAVMF, Bering Collection, Case 66, p. 264.

[36] Bering Expedition, p. 79.

[37] Central States Historical Archives, Leningrad, Collection 1341, Section 303, Cases 485-6, 1764.

[38] William Walton joined the Russian service as a navigator October 23, 1723. On January 18, 1733, at the insistence of Bering, he was assigned to the Second Kamchatka-Pacific Ocean Expedition. He went to Japan as commander of one of the ships in Spanberg's fleet. After reaching $43^0 20$'L. he returned to Bolsheretsk. In the next year, he made another voyage to Japan and reached $33^0 28$'L. In 1741, he participated in the description of the Okhotsk Sea to the east to Ilia River and to the south to Uliia River. On December 4, 1743, he died in Siberia in route from Kamchatka to Moscow. (General Marine Roster, Parts I and II.)

[39] *Russkie otkrytiya v Tikhom okeane Severioy Amerike XVIII veke.* i co vstupitelinoy statiey doktora istorichckikh nauk, A.N. Andreev, St. Petersburg: Geografgiz, 1948, p. 99.

[40] TsGAVMF, Collection 913, Section 2, Case 38, pp. 447 and the other side.

[41] TsGAVMF, Collection 918, Section 2, Case 38, p.449.

[42] On November 4, 1741, the packet-boat *St. Peter* wrecked near one of the Commander Islands. On December 8, Captain-Commander Bering died of scurvy. Many members of the expedition did not survive the winter. Those who did survive built a small ship from the remains of the *St. Peter* and returned to Petropavlovsk the following summer.

[43] TsGADA, Bk 57, pp. 86 and the other side.

[44] Ibid., pp. 97 and the other side.

[45] Shelting, Alexi Elisarovich (Dutch) joined the Russian fleet in 1729. He participated in the voyage from Kronstadt to Arkhangelsk. At his request, he was appointed to the Kam chatka Expedition in 1733. He made three voyages to the Kuril Islands and Japan. He was appointed to the Baltic Fleet soon afterhis return from the expedition. In 1772, he received the rank of Middle-Admiral and retired February 18, 1780.

[46] TsGADA, Admiralty College Collection, Bk 56, p. 488.

[47] TsGAVMF, Bering Collection, Case 56, pp. 60 and the other side.

[48] Ibid., p. 745.

[49] Gvozdev's of September 2, 1743, see A.V. Efimov, *Iz istorii russkikh ekspeditsii no tikhom okeane*, Moscow, 1948, p, 248.

[50] Central States Historical Archives, Leningrad, Collection 1341, Section 303, Cases 485-6, 1764.

III Appendix

Mikhail Gvozdev Petition to the Empress

1

At the end of 1716, by decree I was determined, your servant, to serve in the name of science at the Moscow Academy. I as there until 1719. In that year I was sent the St. Petersburg Academy for the purpose of studying geodesy. I was there until 1721. In that year I was sent to Novgorod to serve under General Mikhail Volkov describing rivers and army infantry camps until September, 1725. I was then sent back to the St. Petersburg Academy. At the end of 1727, being examined by Professor Pharvarson I was qualified as a geodesist. In 1727, I joined the expedition of Captain Pavlutski and Cossack Leader Shestakov. I was in Kamchatka until 1735. In that year I was sent to Tobolsk because of the testimony of sailor Petrov. I was in the Siberian Governor's Chancellery until July, 1738. According to the verdict, I was determined to be innocent of the charges against me. In 1738, according to the decree of the Admiralty College to the Siberian Governor's Chancellery, I was sent from Tobolsk to Okhotsk remaining there until 1741. In that year, by order of Captain Walton, I was sent from Okhotsk to describe the coast of the Okhotsk Sea from the mouth of the Okota River towards Udsk a distance of 200 versts as per the Captain's instructions.

2

After my return in 1741, at Captain Spanberg's request, I joined his expedition and was sent on the double-sloop *Nadezhda* on a voyage with midshipman Shelting to describe the coast from the mouth of the Uda River to the Amur River. And in 1742 I was assigned by midshipman Shelting on the same ship to describe the mouth of the Amur River and its banks. During these voyages I performed my duties willingly and professionally.

3

According to the Senate decree of 1733, in the name of Empress Anna Ivanovna, according to which all geodesists who were assigned to go to Siberia again should be given the rank of Warrant Officer and those who had been sent previously and were still in Siberia - four people and one in Kamchatka - were to be promoted to the rank of Sub-Lieutenant. According to the decree, the Siberian Governor's Chancellery and the Irkutsk Province Chancellery were directed to promote Peter Skobeltsyn, Dmitrii Baskakov, Ivan Svistunov and Basil Shatilov to the rank of Sub-Lieutenant. And those ranks were also sent to them from the State Admiralty College. And I, your servant, still have not been promoted to the rank about which I have been inquiring since July, 1740. I sent my request to the State Admiralty College through Captain Bering and still have not received a response.

Your kindness, Empress, I am asking for assistance. In August, 1743, I am serving under Captain Spanberg. This petition is written by copyist Yakov Dasajev from the crew. And because there is no coat of arms paper for sale

102

in Okhotsk, the request is written on plain paper to which Mikhail Gvozdev adds his signature.

TsGAVMF, Collection 216, Case 56, pp. 966-7.

Testimony of Mikhail Gvozdev
given to Siberian Governor's Chancellery
concerning the voyage to the American coast.

On June 13, 1738, Mikhail Gvozdev in the Siberian Governor's Chancellery says that he was sent from the Admiralty College to be a member of the Kamchatka Expedition with Captain Dmitri Pavlutski and Yakutian Cossack leader Afanacy Shestakov to find new lands and reconcile foreigners who used to be under Russian protection.

In 1728 I was sent from Tobolsk with mariner Fedorov and arrived in Yakutsk in 1729. In July of that year I traveled from Yakutsk to Okhotsk with Captain Pavlutski where I remained until 1730. In that year, by Pavlutski's order, I sailed from Okhotsk on the *St. Gabriel* thorough the Lamskoe Sea to Kamchatka with Yakov Gens. I remained at Bolsheretsk ostrog with Gens until July, 1731, waiting for orders from Pavlutski. After we received the order, we sailed to the mouth of the Kamchatka River. On July 20, the natives rebelled and burned and beat the Russians. That is why Major Merlin and Pavlutski and Gvozdev lived in yurts until 1733 at the mouth of the Kamchatka River with the sailors, ex-sailors and servicemen. Former mariner Fedorov died in 1733. Gregory Skorniakov-Pisarev sent a decree from Okhotsk for navigator Gens to bring the servicemen to Okhotsk ostrog. Gvozdev was directed to go to the Nizhne-

Kamchatsk ostrog. After Pavlutski arrived, Gvozdev was sent to Tobolsk in 1735 because of the testimony of Leonti Petrov but was later found to be innocent. There was no map or journal prepared of the voyage because of the illness and blindness of Gens and the assistant navigator, Fedorov, who died of a foot ailment and Gvozdev could not prepare them by himself alone.

To this true account geodesist Mikhail Gvozdev added his hand.

TsGAVMF, Collection 216, Case 24, pp. 587 and the other side.

The Report of the Secret Adviser and Siberian Governor F.I. Soimonov about Gvozdev's participation in the determining of the Agricultural Reserves in Irkutsk Province and about His Discharge from geodesist's duties because of his illness.

According to the secret decree of your Empress' greatness, received from the Senate on August 18, and in Tobolsk by the former Siberian Governor Admiral-Cavalier Myatlov received October 22, 1754, the description of all lands assigned as residences of runaway farm workers and peoples brought from Poland was ordered. The completed descriptions were to be presented to the Senate. The three remaining geodesists and the former Kamchatka Expedition Sub-Lieutenant of Geodesy Gvozdev and Warrant Officer Chikin from Tomsk were to be used for the descriptions in Irkutsk Province. On about November 5, 1754, the report was sent to the Senate by me, Admiral and Cavalier. That is why, according to your

Empress' decree, there are three geodesists there to describe the land and in Irkutsk Province is Sub-Lieutenant Gvozdev sent from Tomsk to prepare a description of the land from Irkutsk along the Moscow Road in specific locations. In the villages of Urikovski, Kudinski and Oyetski, Gvozdev prepared the descriptions in great pain. Because his eyesight has failed, Gvozdev can no longer do the work of a geodesist. For this reason Gvozdev sent a request to the Irkutsk Chancellery (which was sent to me) asking to be discharged from his duties because of his illness. I reported this to the Senate and requested his retirement and discharge from service because of his illness, age and long service. Since he can no longer perform his duties and hold his position, he can be assigned to projects that he is able to do. And instead of Gvozdev, send another geodesist to finish Irkutsk Province and Nerchinsk District and then work in the Siberia District and Irkutsk Province when he is finished.
 Fedor Soimonov
With additional note,
Dmitri Kolugin
Secretary Basil Lasarev
December 23, 1758

Central State Historical Archives, Leningrad, Collection 1341, Section 303, Case 485, 1764, Part 1, pp. 397-8 and the other side. Original.

V History of the names of the Islands in the Bering Strait

from Goldenberg, L.A., *Mikhail Spiridonovicha Gvozdev*,
Moscow: Nuaka, 1985, pp. 148-156.

Source	Diomede	
	Ratmanov	Kruzenshtren
1. Map "Kamchadal-skaya land Lamsk and Penzhin seas, as were found and inspected as a result of various expeditions by Russian Cossacks and hunters for sable on water and land." (translated from German) From Homman's Atlas, 1725.	"Empty"	"Island where people live"
2. "Map representing Anadyr ostrog and Anadyr Sea" I. Lvov, not earlier that 1727-8 TsGADA, f, 192, Irkutsk Province, #26	"On this island live people, who Chukchi call ahuhalyat"	"On this island live people, who Chukchi call peekeli"
3. "Index to the cities and famous Siberian places..." First Kam-chatka Expedition, 1728. *Bering's Expe-dition*, p. 66.	"Island of St. Dio-mede" $67^0$00'N.L. $125^0$42'E. of Tobolsk	

Islands		
Fairway Rock	King Island	Cape Prince of Wales
-	-	Not names (on a different version of the map: "Incognita.")
-	-	" Land is Big, and there live people, who Chukchi call kiginedyat."
-	-	-

Source	Diomede	
	Ratmanov	Kruzenshtren
4. Reports of Geo-desist M.S. Gvozdev 1741 and September 1, 1743, Efimov, 1948, pp. 236-243 and pp. 244-249.	"First Island"	"Second Island"
5. Map of North-East Asia. Y.I. Lindenau, 1742. TsGADA, f. 248, Maps, No. 1910	Without a name	Without a name
6. "Map Mekatorskaya from Okhotsk to the Chukota Nos...." M.P. Spanberg's Oct. 1743 TsGAVA, f. 192, VUA No. 23431; ATsKP VMF No. 69, 70.	"St. Diomede"	Without a name

Islands		
Fairway Rock	King Island	Cape Prince of Wales
Not named	"Fourth Island"	"Big Land"
Without a name	Without a name	"Big Land"
Without a name	Without a name	"Geodesist Gvozdev was here, 1732"

Source	Ratmanov	Diomede Kruzenshtren
7. "Map of Northern part of the East Ocean with Bering Strait and part of the Arctic Ocean" Naval Academy, 1746. ATsKP, VMF, No.82; see TsGVEA, f. VUA, No. 23466, 20227.	"St. Diomede"	Without a name
8. "Mappa Monde..." G.M. Lovitsa, 1746 from "Atlas von Hundert Carte Atlas Humonnianus, 1773.	-	-
9. Map of Chukotka peninsula and part of Perevalov's Kamchatka, October 1754 Atlas, 1964, No. 124	Island of large-toothed Chukoch	
	"People here"	"On this island live people called large-toothed peekeli"

Islands		
Fairway Rock	King Island	Cape Prince of Wales
Without a name	"Nomand's tent"	(in the legend) "Land, laid across from Chukotka East corner to the east laying from 65^0 to 68^0 N.L. taken from the map of geodesist Gvozdev."
-	-	"detecta a Gwosdew 1730"
-	-	"Island or Big Land and people live here who Chukchi call kiginedyat"

Source	Diomede Ratmanov	Kruzenshtren
10. Map of G.F. Muller, 1754-1758 "Nouvelle carta des decouvertes, faites par des vaisseaux Russiens aux cotes inconnues de l'Amerique Septentrionale avec les pays adjacents" TsGADA, f. 192, Irkurtsk Province, No. 50	" I. St. Diomede ᠌	-
"A Map of the Discoveries made by the Russians on the Northwest coast of America" London, 1761	The same	-
11. Map of North-eastern Asia pointing out existing and planned sea and land routes. F.I. Soimonov, 1760 TsGADA, f. 248, maps, No. 1911 Rough draft of this map in TsGVEA, Efimov, 1958, il. 4.	"Diomede Island"	-

Islands		
Fairway Rock	King Island	Cape Prince of Wales
-	-	"Cote decouverte par le geodesiste Gwosdew 1730"
		"Coast Discovered by surveyor Gvozdev in 1730"
-	-	"Land western part of America, to which in 1732 Gvozdev has been to, exactness of which is not known"

Source	Diomede Ratmanov	Diomede Kruzenshtren
12. "Map of Province of Yakutsk, Chukota land, Kamchatka land with nearby places and part of America with nearby islands" Perevalov's, not earlier than 1763 "Red Archives," 1936 T. 1, p. 160.	"Magli Island. Large-toothed Chukchi live here"	"Igali Island Large-toothed Chukchi live here"
13. "Map of Chukota Land with part of American shore" Daurkin, 1765. TsGVEA, f.VUA, No. 23435.	(Abridged) "Imyuaglin Island. There large toothed people live"	(Abridged) "Inyallin Island. There live same people as on Imyuaglin"
14. "Map of Eastern Asia. Vertlugov, 1767. Coxe, 1780, p. 322; Alexandrov, No. 104.	Without a name	Without a name

Islands		
Fairway Rock	King Island	Cape Prince of Wales
Without a name	Without a name	"Part of North America. Live here people called kuhkmultsami"
(Abridged) "Empty Is. called Okivahai"	(Abridged) "Okiben Island. There live the same people as on the Big Land"	Cape Prince
Without a name	-	"Big Land"

117

Source	Ratmanov	Diomede Kruzenshtren
15. "Map of Yakutsk Province, Kamchatka and Anadyr River with nearby Chukota land, also part of N. America and Japan." Perevalov, not earlier than 1767. TsGADA, f. 192 Irkutsk Prov #10	"Magli Island. Large toothed Chukchi live here"	"Ogalgi Island. Large toothed Chukchi live here"
16. "Map of Northeastern Asia and North America" F. Plenisnera, around 1770, Alexandrov, No.123, Atlas 1964, No. 131.	"First Inyalin Island, people live on it"	"Second Inyalin Island, people live on it"
17. "Map which shows discoveries of Russian seamen on Northern part of America with nearby places on various voyages which occurred." I.F. Truskott - G.F. Muller 1773. AAN, p. IX, op.la, No. 210; ATsKP VMP, No. 86.	-	-

Islands		
Fairway Rock	King Island	Cape Prince of Wales
Without a name	Without a name	"Land discovered during geodesist Gvozdev's voyage from Kamchatka"
"Child without a home Okivahai"	Without a name	"Land called Kygmyn"
-	-	"Coast discovered by geodesist Gvozdev in 1730"

Source	Ratmanov	Diomede Kruzenshtren
18. Copy of N. Daurkin's map (1765) with reviewed explanation, 1774. TsGADA, f.199, portf. 539, p.1, d. 1a, l. 20.	"Imaglin Island"	"Inyalin Island"
19. "Chart of Norton Sound and Bering Strait..." Cook and Clerke, 1778-1779, (Published in English 1782, 1784, 1785)	-	-
20. "Map belonging to sotnik Ivan Kobelev's voyages" 1779 *Meshyatsolov Historical and Geographical,* St. Petersburg, 1784.	"Imahlin"	"Igellin"
Handwritten version of the map of I. Kobelev's voyage in 1779. Federov, 1971, ill. 1.	"Imaglin Island"	"Igellin Island"

Islands		
Fairway Rock	King Island	Cape Prince of Wales
"Empty Okivahai Island"	"Okiban Island"	"...Big Land, part of America, and called in Chukchi language Kygmyn"
-	"King"	"Cape Prince of Wales"
Usien"	-	"American Nos was discovered by geodesist Gvozdev in 1732 and named Gigmalskaya land"
"Ukzen"	-	"Nos of America, which was previously known in 1730 by name of Kygmalskaya by geodesist Gvozdev"

To the American Coast

Source	Ratmanov	Diomede Kruzenshtren
21. Map of 1781 from the "Collection of various maps indicating route to Arctic Ocean and America" AVPR f. 339, op 88 No. 930/10; TsGVEA, f. VUA, No.23741, i.1	Without a name	Without a name
22. "Eastern portion of Irkutsk Province with nearby island and Western coast of America" Vilbrekht, 1787. All names are repeated without changes in Russian and French publications of the "maps showing the discoveries by Russian seamen in the Pacific Ocean and English Captain Cook" A.M. Vilbrekht, 1787. TswGVIA. f. VUA, No. 23780, 23758	Without a name	Without a name

Islands		
Fairway Rock	King Island	Cape Prince of Wales
Without a name	-	"American Nos, on which Gvozdev has been in 1732"
Without a name	King Island	"C. Prince of Wales. This nos was already known in 1732 geod. Gvozdev by name Kigmalskaya Land"

To the American Coast

Source	Diomede	
	Ratmanov	Kruzenshtren
23. "Merkatorskaya map, indicating Arctic Ocean, Bering Strait and part of the Eastern Ocean with the coast of Chukota land and North America" Sarichev, 1791. Sarichev, 1802 Atlas, i. 52.	"Gvozdev Islands"	
24. Merkatorskaya map of Bering Strait" Kotsebue, 1816. Kotzebue, 1821.	Ratmanov	Gvozdev Kruzenshtern
25. Merkatorskaya map, indicating Arctic Ocean, Bering Strait and part of the Eastern Ocean with coast of Chukota Land and North America" M.N. Vasilev and F.P.Wrangell, 1821. AVPR, f. 339, op. 888, No. 949/29; TsGVEA, f. VUA, No. 23424.	Without a name	Gvozdev Without a name

Islands		
Fairway Rock	King Island	Cape Prince of Wales
"Kivahoi"	"Okiben"	"Cape of Kigmile Village"

Islands	"King"	"Cape Prince of Wales"
Without a name		

Islands	-	"Cape Prince of Wales"
Without a name		

Source	Diomede	
	Ratmanov	Kruzenshtren
26. "Map of Russian possessions in N. America" V.N . Berkh, 1821, ATsKP, VMP, No. 188.	Without a name	Without a name

Source		Gvozdev
27. "General map of Bering Sea" and "Ignaluk" "Merkatorskaya map of Western coast of Bering Strait, made from description of Fleet-Captain F. Litke from the sloop *Sinya-vine*, 1828, Litke, 1835, Atlas, I. 1,2.	"Nunarbook"	

Source	Gvozdev Islands or St.	
28. "Meratorskaya general map of part of Russian possessions in America" L.A. Zagoskin, 1844 (Published in 1848) Zagoskin, 1956, appendix	"Imaklit Island"	"Inaklit Island"

Islands		
Fairway Rock	King Island	Cape Prince of Wales
Without a name	Without a name	"Cape described by Gvozdev in 1732"

Islands	"King's Island"	"Cape Prince of Wales"
"Ukiyok"		

Diomedes	"Ukivok Island"	"Cape of Nihta Village or Cape Prince of Wales"
"Ukiyok Island"		

To the American Coast

Source	Diomede	
	Ratmanov	Kruzenshtren
29. Sea Atlas,	"Diomede(Gvozdev's)	
1950-1958	Ratmanov	Kruzenshtren
	Island	Island
	-Big	-Little
	Diomede	Diomede
	-Imaklit	65^045'N.L.
	-Nurarbook	168^055'W.L
	65^045'N.L.	
	169^000'W.L.	

Islands		
Fairway Rock	King Island	Cape Prince of Wales
"Fairway Rock"	"King Island"	"Cape Prince of Wales"
$65^0 45$'N.L.	$64^0 59$'N.L.	$65^0 35$'N.L.
$168^0 45$'W.L.	$168^0 01$'W.L.	$168^0 05$'W.L.

VI Bibliography for Introduction

Andreev, I. *The Destiny of Russian America 1741-1867.*
ed. R.A. Pierce & trans. M. Ramsey, Kingston and
Fairbanks: The Limestone Press 1990.

Bagrow, L. "Ivan Kirilov, Compiler of the First Russian
Atlas, 1689-1737." *Imaga Mundi*, II 1938.

Baker J.N.L. *A History of Geographical Discovery and
Exploration.* Boston: Houghton Mifflin Co., 1931.

Baker, M. *Geographic Dictionary of Alaska.* Washington:
Government Printing Office, 1906.

Berhk, V.N. *A Chronological History of the Discovery of
the Aleutian Islands.* ed. R.A. Pearce, trans. D.
Krenov, Kingston, Ontario: The Limestone Press,
1974.

Bancroft, H.H. *History of Alaska.* New York: The
Bancroft Company, 1886.

Black, J.L. *G.-F. Muller and the Imperial Russian
Academy.* Kingston and Montreal: McGill-
Queen's University Press, 1986.

Brebner, J.B. *The Explorers of North America 1492-1806.*
London: A&C Black Ltd., 1933.

Breitfuss, L. "Early Maps of North-Eastern Asia and
of the Lands around the North Pacific:
Controversy Between G.F. Muller and N. Delisle."
Imago Mundi, III, 1939, pp.87-99.

Burney, J. *Chronological History of North-Eastern
Voyages of Discovery and of the Early Eastern
Navigations of the Russians.* London: Payne and
Foss, 1819.

Coxe, W. *A Comparative View of the Russian Discoveries with those made by Captains Cook and Clerke.* London: J. Nichols, 1787.

Dall, W.H. *Alaska and Its Resources.* Boston: Lee and Shepard, 1870.

Divin, V.A. *K beregam Ameriki. Plavaniya i issledovaniya M. S. Gvozdeva, pervootkryvatelya Severo-Zpadnoy Ameriki,* Moscow: Geografgiz, 1956.

Dmytryshyn, B. Crownhart-Vaughan, E.A.P., Vaughan, T. ed. and trans., *Russian Penetration of the North Pacific Ocean 1700-1797.* Portland: Oregon Historical Society Press, 1988.

Dobbs, A. ed. *A Letter from a Russian Sea-Officer, to a Person of Distinction at the Court of St. Petersburgh.* London: A. Linde, etc., 1754

Falk, M.W. *Alaska.* World bibliograpical series; V. 183. Oxford, England; Santa Barbara Calif.: CLIO Press, 1995.

Fisher, R.H. *Bering's Voyages: Whither and Why.* Seattle and London: University of Washington Press, 1977.

Fisher, R.H. "The Early Carography of the Bering Strait Region," *Arctic,* Vol. 37, No. 4, Dec., 1984

Frost, O.W. ed., *Bering and Chirikov: The American Voyages and Their Impact.* Anchorage: Alaska Historical Society, 1992

Goldenberg, L.A. *Katorzhanin--sibirskii gubernator: zhizn' i trudy F.I. Soimonova.* Magadan: Magadan Publishing House, 1979.

Goldenberg, L.A. "'Geodesist Gvozdev was Here in 1732' (Eighteenth Century Cartographic Traditions in the Representation of the Discovery of Bering Strait." in *Polar Geography and Geology*, Vol. 7, July-Sept. 1983, pp.214-223.

Goldenberg, L.A. *Gvozdev: The Russian Discovery of Alaska in 1732.* ed. J.L.Smith, trans.N.M. Phillips and A.M. Perminov, Anchorage: Whitestone Press, 1990.

Golder, F.A. *Russian Expansion on the Pacific 1641-1850.* Cleveland: The Arthur H. Clark Co., 1914

Golder, F.A. *Berings Voyages.* New York: Octagon Books, Inc., 1968, (originally published in 1922 by the American Geographical Society of New York).

Heawood, E. *A History of Geographical Discovery in the Seventeenth and Eighteenth Centuries.* New York: Octagon Books 1969 (reprint of 1912 edition published by Cambridge University Press).

Hulley, C.C. *Alaska: Past and Present.* Portland: Binfords & Mort, 1970.

Hunt, W. *Arctic Passage.* New York: Charles Scribner's Sons, 1975.

Khisamutdimov, A.A. "The Route of the St. Peter to America," in *Bering and Chirikov: The American Voyages and Their Impact.* ed. O.W. Frost, Anchorage: Alaska Historical Society, 1992. p. 163.

Krashninnikov, S.P. *Explorations of Kamchatka, 1735-1741.* Trans. E.A.P. Crownhart-Vaughan, Portland: Oregon Historical Society, 1972.

To the American Coast

Lanzeff, G.V. and Richard A. Pierce. *Eastward to Empire: Exploration and conquest on the Russian Open Frontier, to 1750.* Montreal: McGill-Queen's University Press, 1973.

Makarova, R.V. *Russians in the Pacific, 1743-1799.* Ed. and trans. by R.A. Pierce and A.S. Donnelly, Kingston: The Limestone Press, 1975.

Muller, G.F. *Bering's Voyages: The Reports from Russia.* trans, C.L. Urness, University of Alaska Press: Fairbanks, 1986.

Polevoy, B.P. "The 250th Anniversary of the Discovery of Alaska." in *Polar Geography and Geology*, Vol. 7, July-Sept. 1983, pp.205-213.

Ray, D.J. *The Eskimos of Bering Strait, 1650-1898.* Seattle and London: University of Washington Press, 1975, also see 1992 edition.

Robertson, W. *The History of America.* London: W. Strahan; T. Cadell, 1777, Bk. IV.

Shopotov, K.A., "The Year 1992 is the 260th Anniversary of the Russian Discovery of Alaska." in *Bering and Chirikov: The American Voyages and Their Impact.* ed. O.W. Frost. Anchorage: Alaska Historical Society, 1992.

Svet, Y.M. and S.G. Fedorova, "Captain Cook and the Russians," in *Pacific Studies.* VI, No. 1, Fall 1978. pp. 1-19.

Urness, C.L. "Bering's First Expedition: A Re-examination Based on Eighteenth-century Books, Maps, and Manuscripts." Ph.D dissertation, University of Minnesota, 1982.

135